Public Education Is a Sacred Calling

Public Education Is a Sacred Calling

Citizen Stakeholders All—For the Common Good!

THEODORE V. FOOTE JR.

RESOURCE *Publications* · Eugene, Oregon

PUBLIC EDUCATION IS A SACRED CALLING
Citizen Stakeholders All—For the Common Good!

Resource Publications
An Imprint of Wipf and Stock Publishers
199 W. 8th Ave., Suite 3
Eugene, OR 97401

www.wipfandstock.com

PAPERBACK ISBN: 978-1-4982-9733-2
HARDCOVER ISBN:978-1-4982-9735-6
EBOOK ISBN: 978-1-4982-9734-9

Manufactured in the U.S.A.   SEPTEMBER 12, 2016

Contents

Acknowledgments | vii

1   The Sum of Varied Resources, Especially People! | 1

2   Sacred Calling Challenges as Part of the Quest | 7

3   A Primer for Citizen Stakeholders | 12

4   Mentioning "The Main Thing" and "There Are No Do-Overs" | 18

5   "Public" Is the Main Thing | 25

6   Varied Education Trajectories | 34

7   Approach-Perspectives to Twelve Challenge Topics | 47

8   Eleven Questions Related to Public Education for the Common Good | 63

Epilogue and Afterword | 99

Appendicies

A   Developing a Compatible Rationale for Public Ethics and Cooperative Service among Both Religious and Non-Religious Persons | 105

B   Qualitative Interview Process and Demographics | 110

C   Outline Diagram for Chapter 6, Varied Education Trajectories | 113

CONTENTS

D   Outline Diagram for Chapter 7, Approach-Perspectives to Twelve Challenge Topics | 114

E   List of Questions for Chapter 8, Eleven Questions Related to Public Education for the Common Good | 115

Bibliography | 117

Index | 125

Acknowledgments

I OWE PARTICULAR AND unending gratitude to The Louisville Institute for the endorsement, conversation, and funding that turned this effort from a proposal into a genuine project effort.

I am grateful more than words can express: (1) to my parents, who benefited from public education in the 1930s and -40s; (2) to Dr. James Burk, Dr. Rick Avery, Dr. Walter Buenger, and Dr. Victoria Buenger for local mentoring and support; (3) to the Session Elders and members of First Presbyterian Church, Bryan, Texas, among them my clergy colleague, the Reverend Marie Mickey; to other staff members, most notably, Karen Berg (our office coordinator), for negotiating time slots and taking up slack I often created related to this project; (4) to the Sisters of the Congregation of Divine Providence in residence on the campus of Our Lady of the Lake University (San Antonio), who hospitably allowed this Protestant clergyperson a retreat site for a week of focused effort to draw the manuscript into completed form; (5) to Nicole McKinley, Dr. Robert Baker, and Dr. Nancy Self, who read the first draft of the manuscript and offered substantive organizational critiques; (6) to the forty-plus "stewards of education" across eight states who generously granted interview time to an outsider they had not met before, who was asking to hear their respective stories for a project he could not very clearly define for himself, let alone explain to them, and for twenty-plus more who answered questionnaires in lieu of a sit-down interview; (7) to the faculty, staff, and administration of public schools in Gatesville, San Antonio, Austin, Henderson, and Bryan, Texas, and in Tulsa, Oklahoma (where one or more members of the Foote household attended public schools, and/or, as in my spouse's case, served as a faculty member), who have helped shape for me a vision appreciative of public education's contributions, uphill struggles, and continuing potential; and (8) to the Presbyterian Church (USA) and its predecessor bodies, the Presbyterian Church in the United States and the United Presbyterian Church in the United States of America, that have been faith-community examples of the Reformed Christian tradition older than this nation's independence—with an evolving and enduring, non-sectarian commitment to public education.

All of these here mentioned and others unnamed, either personally or from influence at a distance, have "lived a witness" and have given assistance to me, largely due to their shared belief that something positive does occur through public education and might result from an effort of this nature. They have at least given a fleeting thought that some contribution to the common good might materialize, both in the present and the future, for younger and older girls and boys and for women and men of all backgrounds and in multiple contexts and types of communities across the democratic republic we call the United States of America.

Mentioned last in my inventory of indebtedness, yet always enduring and sharing most acutely the commitments of an effort like this, are my spouse and best friend, Joanie, and—at a distance—our two adult sons, Kendall and Payton.

No one, of course, is responsible for any errors of omission, commission, mischaracterization, or inaccuracy except for me, for which I shall both now and later extend sincere apologies, whether such errors are called to my attention sooner, later, or never.

Chapter 1

The Sum of Varied Resources, Especially People!

I AM AN OUTSIDER. As I write this, as far as public education (grades pre-kindergarten through twelve) is concerned, I am not a student, a parent, a grandparent, an educator, an administrator, a legislator, a government education official, a professional education consultant, or an educators' association staff person.

I do have a personal history and set of connections with public education. I am a product of twelve years of public education (1959–71). I am the parent of two sons, each with thirteen years as public school students (high school graduates in 2005 and 2010), and my spouse has been a public school classroom educator for more than thirty years.

I offer the preceding qualifying information both as a disclaimer and as a statement of full disclosure. Such contexts and connections having been stated, I hope to eliminate the possibility of particular criticisms that would be legitimately based on my failure to reveal this, and which would lower the credibility of the conclusions herein advanced.

When this project was only a seed of an idea, I fully realized I was an outsider. There's a saying related to this, and, unfortunately, it can be said of more people than those who are only beginners, rookies, or novices, and absolutely it can be said of those with less experience than others: "You don't even know what you don't know."

This certainly was true of me at the outset of this project, and still is in many respects. It's an important characteristic to cultivate—awareness of the limitations of one's knowledge and experience—so that one does not venture in where fools (should) fear to tread.[1]

In proposing a project to explore whether nonsectarian religious values might healthily intersect with the realities and dynamics of US public education, I at least had the good sense to request funding both for travel to conduct interviews in diverse locations across the United States and for books so I could read up on what experts and those steeped in education efforts had thought in the past and are still recently thinking, writing, evaluating, and advancing as research results or refined and revised ideas and practices.

It has been said in various contexts, "A leader is only as good as her or his teammates, colleagues, workers," and other associates. I have come to believe this of public education through the exploration of this topic, whether I realized this in theory before I began, or not.

Education, including public education, is only as capable of positive outcomes as the sum of the people who invest themselves professionally, along with the people who invest themselves as a corporate, societal, broad community and public. This sum effort is three-fold: (1) in support of the current students; (2) in support of the current education professionals and auxiliary staff; and (3) in support of the best possible future "beyond us" (which always begins tomorrow). The sum of every day's potential for public education with every student is determined significantly by citizen investments and involvement in the present.

Garrison Keillor has said about the citizens of his fictional Minnesota hamlet on the northern prairie: "People are in favor of education, at least in principle, in Lake Wobegon."[2] Keillor's

---

1. Paraphrased from Pope, *An Essay on Criticism*, Part III.
2. Keillor, *Prairie Home Companion*, February 2, 2015.

tongue-in-cheek humor and wit (both of which sail in the boat of understatement) accurately convey how education "in principle" will not suffice. While all is going well, education "in principle" leads to the unspoken conclusion and the spoken rationale that when any train actually jumps the tracks in the public education realm, whatever is wrong is someone else's fault, and likely someone else's responsibility to fix.

In her 2014 volume, *The Teacher Wars: A History of America's Most Embattled Profession*, Dana Goldstein writes, "Anxiety about bad teaching is understandable."[3] She continues, "In the Obama era, the predominant policy response to . . . very real problems [in public education] has been a narrow one: to weaken teachers' tenure protections and then use 'measures of student learning'—a euphemism for children's scores on an ever-expanding battery of hastily designed tests—to identify and fire bad teachers."[4]

Goldstein writes those sentences early in her book and then devotes 272 pages to writing a history of public education as related to professional personnel, mostly classroom educators. She reports from her observations: "Watching a great teacher at work can feel like watching a magic show."[5] Of course, not all classroom educators are by nature, by skill development, or by virtue of situation in settings where they shine from class period to class period, like renowned magicians. Goldstein quotes a Denver, Colorado, area teacher who likely speaks for others, not in condemnation of professional standards debates, but in the midst of them: "A lot of the discourse is about getting rid of bad teachers. Very rarely do I perceive teachers as anything other than cogs in a machine . . . [This work needs to be] challenging and stimulating to adults. I am an intelligent person who has this love and passion for educating kids. So let me use what I know to create an experience for my students that reflects my expertise."[6]

3. Goldstein, *The Teacher Wars*, 2.
4. Ibid.
5. Ibid, 244.
6. Ibid., 261–62.

Dana Goldstein is a professional journalist. I am not in her league any more than I am an education insider. As a part of the research for this book, during the dozens of interviews in multiple states I was privileged to conduct with education insiders and stakeholders, I heard and learned much about the joys and challenges experienced by those who are part of the endeavor and enterprise of public education (cf. appendix B). Nothing I was told face-to-face in the field contradicted anything I read either in Goldstein's book or in related books and articles that I studied following the interviews. Everything teachers, administrators, parents, and other education-related employees, volunteers, elected officials, or consultants said seemed consistent with what I subsequently read: Where they had described conflicts, difficulties, and discouragement, the literature may have reflected or argued from a variety of opinions, but the reality of up-hill struggles is candidly acknowledged. Where those in the field described fulfillment and positive developments and engagements in the endeavor of public education and its duties, the literature (again) described the same.

The field interviews allowed me on-site encounters and real-life/real-time glimpses into four respective worlds: (1) that of educators in the classrooms and conference rooms of facilities that ran the gamut from deteriorating stone, brick, and mortar structures 100 or more years old to vinyl-covered, wooden portables, to shiny new brick and glass facilities; (2) that of administrators in their offices and on their campuses; (3) that of education agency representatives, education consultants, and activists in their areas and locales of responsibility; and (4) that of parents in communities where schools play such major roles in the lives of their sons and daughters.

Hearing from these constituencies in person provided a standard against which to test and measure all that I would read and digest in the weeks and months following the interviews themselves (please see the bibliography at the end of this book). I am still an outsider to the enterprise and endeavor of public education, but many professional and stakeholder participants have coached me up through revealing their personal and professional passion, commitment, and learnings, both in conversation and by way of print.

In their book with a title dripping with sarcasm, *Teachers Have It Easy: The Big Sacrifices and Small Salaries of America's Teachers*, Daniel Moulthrop, Ninive Clements Calegari, and Dave Eggers write: "Teachers are not the only cost in education, nor are they the only important cost in education. But good teaching is one of the factors that has the most important influence in student achievement and is the one factor that can counteract the forces of low socioeconomic status, despite how powerful and predictive those forces can be."[7]

Several pages later they conclude:

> If we want to attract exceptional people to the teaching profession, we must pay them substantially more . . . It doesn't take superheroes to make this happen. It simply demands that people take risks. It demands that our elected representatives be forward thinking, creative, and willing to truly support educators and those who run school districts . . . Communities must be vocal about how important good teaching is to them. People must be clear that spending money to find, keep, and support the best teachers is simply the most effective investment they can make in the future of their children, their communities, and their country.[8]

Public education resources vary from neighborhood to neighborhood, community to community, and state to state. In every locale, persons reside in and comprise a public. As I have said, public education is only as capable of positive outcomes as the sum of the people who invest themselves professionally, of students, semester-by-semester, and of the people who invest themselves as a public made up of citizen stakeholders, all of whom support the students, the education community employees, and the future— those who come after us—doing so with positive involvement

7. Moulthrop, et al., *Teachers Have It Easy*, 282.

8. Ibid., 286–87.

and stewardship (of heart, mind, body, strength, time, talent, and finances) in the present.

In *The Last Dropout: Stop the Epidemic*, Bill Millican writes:

> There are millions of young people in our schools who are close to giving up. They're desperately searching for a future. By coming together as a community in and around our schools, we have the capacity and the resources (slightly paraphrasing a former U.S. Department of Education theme) "to leave no child behind" . . . [May] we all have new minds to think differently, not simply to try harder – that we may develop "magic eyes" to see the incredible assets already in place throughout our schools and communities. And may our hearts be filled with love that never quits until there truly is hope and a future for our children.[9]

Of all resources that may be available to a school or school district, the people who comprise the public as stakeholders—(a) those on the districts' payrolls; (b) those enrolled as students (plus their parents and care-givers); and (c) those residing as (non-student, non-educator, non-district-staff-employee) members of the community any given day—are the very resources most important to public education as an endeavor both on that given day and beyond. They are all resources, yes, and more. They are all potential contributors to one another, today as well as in the todays which are yet to be, both as they are consciously remembered and as their influence is positively yet subconsciously internalized and appropriated in other relationships far beyond the classrooms, labs, rehearsal halls, athletic settings, and other places where initial learnings occur and seeds of knowledge are planted and nurtured.

9. Milliken, *The Last Dropout*, 200.

Chapter 2

Sacred Calling Challenges as Part of the Quest

To justify a title like *Public Education Is a Sacred Calling* necessitates some unpacking and exploration. The term "sacred calling" can be nonsectarian and even religion-less if one understands (1) "sacred" as an adjective describing "highest value" or "revered endeavor," and (2) "calling" as a noun related to life purpose. For clarification, the word "calling" is derived from the Latin word for "vocation," which is different from "occupation." As an example, being employed as a classroom educator is an "occupation." Every person who is a citizen-stakeholder is also "called" to the vocation of public education as an endeavor, enterprise, and even responsibility of the entire public. So we all share this calling or vocation, whether employed for a pay-check by a school district, a state department of education, or another official education entity, or whether no income at all is received from one's contributions.

One of two crucial aspects of "sacred calling" is personal caring for others, for self, and for service (by one's self) among all others.

The second crucial aspect of "sacred calling" is becoming equipped for citizen stewardship. This includes the aggregate efforts that contribute in any way, shape, and form to the content and goal(s) of public education: from paying school property taxes to serving as volunteer math or reading tutors; from sponsoring a free (or not-for-profit) neighborhood after-school program to participating in a parent-teacher organization or a public education advocacy group; from serving on a school board task force to driving a school bus; from participating in conferences with the teachers of one's children to giving gentle, supportive assistance for homework or project assignments. Citizen stewardship is part of the wide-as-an-ocean pool of resources that contributes to and facilitates public education. Any reward or gain citizen stewards receive is non-monetary, just as when supervisors or friends say to a volunteer receiving no salary or stipend, "If you'll serve in the additional role of _____ (fill in the blank with a duty of your imagination), they'll double (or triple) your pay!" The compensation for citizen stewardship is always non-monetary!

Dana Goldstein selected an 1895 quote from John Dewey to preface *The Teacher Wars*: "It is . . . advisable that the teacher should understand, and even be able to criticize, the general principles upon which the whole educational system is formed and administered. He/she is not like a private soldier in an army expected merely to obey, or like a cog in a wheel, expected merely to respond to and transmit external energy; he/she must be an intelligent medium of action."[1]

As Goldstein begins her book with the permission—even the mandate—for positive education systems to value constructive input, critiques, and initiatives from teachers and other classroom educators, she concludes the book with an insightful commentary on the limits of the United States' public education system, noting how "radically decentralized" our system is when compared with nations in Europe and Asia. She writes: "Unique among Western nations, our national government does not produce or select high quality tests, textbooks, or reading lists for teachers to use . . . [yet] we consistently expect teachers and schools to close achievement gaps and [we] panic when they fail to do so . . . We also do not

1. Goldstein, *The Teacher Wars*, iv (epigraph).

provide families with the full range of social supports children need to thrive academically . . ."[2] Discussing how a decentralized system needs "bridging instruments" between policy and practice, she essentially laments how classroom educators likely will continue to be blamed for the system's limitations unless the public comprehends those limits and why and how they exist.

Even so, her concluding comment is encouraging: "We can move toward a future in which sustainable and transformable education reforms are seeded from the ground up, not imposed from the top down. They will be built more on the expertise of the best teachers than on our fears of the worst teachers."[3] Goldstein's discussion of the US public education's "system's limitations" is an observation she makes from "negative" to "positive," given her hope that a set of responses by public acceptance of such limitations will create an ethos for continual positive (even transformative) developments from that context of limitations.

While Goldstein makes a case for understanding "system limitations" and responding with appropriate strategies and tactics from the ground up while being cognizant of the system's limitations, Parker Palmer encourages individual educators (and, I would add, all citizen stakeholders) to "help our students understand what it means to live and work with the question of an undivided life always before them."[4]

Palmer's encouragement for educators (and the public) to seek, to live by, and to model for others, including students, an "undivided life" is a concluding admonition related to every individual's spiritual and psychological inner compass, authenticity, and/or foundation (my terms). This, he clearly states earlier in his book, never should imply that an individual can achieve perfection of his or her inner compass, authenticity, or foundation before being qualified to serve as a mentor to others. All persons can, he believes, grow to live with the question of the undivided life before them, exemplifying for others this personal quest (and question): "How do I stay close to the

2. Ibid., 273–74.
3. Ibid.
4. Palmer, *The Courage To Teach*, 211.

passions and commitments that took me into this work, challenging myself, and my colleagues, and the institution I work in to keep faith with this profession's deepest values?"[5]

To the extent educators are aware of and engaged in this quest, Palmer is convinced that students will learn and grow their way beyond what is unfortunately frequently taught, by word and example: how one "stays safe by keeping quiet." Rather, he encourages, "Opening one's mouth to challenge what is wrong is a way to stay sane"![6]

These words Palmer wrote in 1998, mostly for professional educators (and which I think crucial to extrapolate to all citizen-stakeholders who are the public) are related to words John Dewey wrote seventy-two years earlier: "The essential need . . . is the improvement of the methods and condition of debate, discussion, and persuasion. That is the problem of the public . . . Inquiry may devolve upon technical experts . . . It is not necessary that 'the many' should have the knowledge and skill to carry on the needed investigations [which "experts" do]; what is required is that they (the public) have the ability to judge of the bearing of the knowledge supplied by others upon common concerns . . . Democracy must begin at home, and its home is the neighborly community . . ."[7]

Dewey is convinced that "the public's most urgent problem is to find and identify itself." To the extent that such a quest is embraced and undertaken, "a fullness, variety, and freedom" will be experienced and witnessed as "alive and flexible, as well as stable and responsive," all the while that meaningful challenges are engaged.[8]

I would add of the public and this sacred calling: the whole is always greater than the sum of the parts; but the whole is always evolving and dynamic and is never a complete end or static, final product.

William Ayers is writing to teachers specifically (and, arguably, to us all) when he asserts: "We claim to be giving students key skills and knowledge, and yet we deny them the one thing that is essential

5. Ibid., 211.
6. Ibid., 212.
7. Dewey, *The Public and Its Problems*, 208–9, 213.
8. Ibid., 216.

to their survival: something to live for . . . When we, as teachers, recognize that we are partners with our students in life's long and complex journey, when we treat them with the dignity and respect they deserve for simply being, then we are on the road to becoming worthy teachers. It's just that simple—and just that difficult."[9]

Public education is a sacred calling wherein individuals can be honored, contexts can be considered, inquiry and debates can be encouraged, and sacrifices can be made. Though we are never perfect, and though we never arrive at a complete end, to the extent that we engage with all others as mutual citizen stewards, the quest toward an undivided life is underway. On such as this, our democracy hinges—all the time.

9. Ayers, *To Teach*, 133.

Chapter 3

A Primer for Citizen Stakeholders

WHILE I AM (AS I wrote in chapter 1) an outsider in terms of formal professional education training, experience, and expertise, I can claim unapologetically and gladly that I am a citizen in the magnificent—although never perfect—democratic republic that is the United States of America. As a citizen, I am a stakeholder in this nation and, therefore, a partner with others in our overall life together as citizens. Since it goes without saying that citizens in this democracy are entitled to respective opinions that vary from those of other citizens, this book never asserts that public education is the sole method or institution by which all students should or can be educated.

This book, rather, unapologetically explores how public education is a fundamental institutional responsibility of the liberal democratic republic and society that is the United States of America, into which we have together evolved, and in which we continue to exist in the first quarter of the twenty-first century.

Here four terms should be defined:

1. "Institution" is a set of interrelated and supportive structures—sociological, economic, political, and others—that function for the provision and governance of services and relationships toward

broad and/or specific goals (which may be negotiated or to which general consent may have been given);

2. "Liberal" is a philosophical adjective, not a political adjective or noun, that means "purposefully expansive and generous in nature";

3. "Democratic" and

4. "republic"—the first an adjective and the second a noun—also have philosophical meaning, both indicating a general form of citizen-participatory and citizen-representative government: a political typology and a citizen-sustained tradition and institution that functions (at best) not impersonally or self-centeredly, but with a view toward the personhood of individuals and their associations as communities.

These terms, therefore, have no partisan association or identification either with the Democrats and the Democratic Party, or with the Republicans and the Republican Party, and are here used to describe a form and institution of government functioning through officials who are elected or appointed to serve: (a) as leader-participants by and through the consent of the governed; and (b) as partners with the governed fellow-citizens themselves, shoulder-to-shoulder in community endeavors and challenges.

Citizen stakeholders—such as each one of us is with others—are essential to an ongoing liberal democratic institutional endeavor like public education; and public education depends on citizen stakeholders who are engaged across geopolitical boundaries as tireless supporters, visionary volunteers, articulate advocates, constructive critics, and astute policy activists. Without citizen stakeholders' involvement at levels that invigorate and propel positive emotional energy and personal, corporate, public, material, and intellectual resources, this institutional endeavor will lose energy, momentum, imagination, innovation, health, and strength.

Given these considerations, there's no reason to apologize for myself or any other person being an outsider if one is an engaged citizen stakeholder seeking the common good. I, along with all others, need to be up front about my own personal life situation, status, and context. Having been trained and employed for close to forty years as a Presbyterian church pastor, I also acknowledge explicitly a particular value assertion that I am now certain has been, for decades, creating awe within me, yet which I mostly sensed only implicitly: that public education is a sacred calling.

It would be easy to dismiss a values-related claim and assertion of this type, given my occupation and professional classification as religious clergy. Some might say: "First, clerical-religious and professional leaders of faith traditions are continually attempting to impose their values on someone else; and, secondly, in the United States, we practice a separation of state and religion that forbids a religious values basis from asserting a shaping influence in public school issues."

There will be no defensive argument from me on the first count. The imposition of religious values is a sectarian practice that, amid a given political milieu, can occur even through endorsing governmental agencies' official policies or practices; and such practice can be routine, customary, or exceptional. This occurs in any society or culture where persons and groups interact on a project or goal of this type, gain a foothold of power, and are able to leverage the system from a given position of influence.

Broadly speaking, "sectarian" refers to religious groups whose faith tenets and beliefs consider their own group as primary and both deserving of and receiving greater favor with God and society (this may be potentially understood as a favored status without God, if the sectarianism is secularist in nature and practice). Such sectarian practices are undertaken because their adherents believe that others—outside of their own (or God's) chosen group—are second-class at best. Sectarians, unless converted, cannot affirm that others who are different in very many ways from themselves might be accepted by God as much as they themselves believe they are accepted by God. Sectarian beliefs and practices express perspectives that are almost exclusively either dismissive, condescending, or repressive of the rights of those who do not share the views of the sectarian-leveraging group.

For example, during the first several years of the current century, various news media reported concerns by some that the United States Air Force Academy had been influenced by the religious values and pressures of neo-evangelical, literalist, exclusivistic, and sectarian Christians.[1] Such reporting has attempted to make the case that this occurs even though the policies of the US Armed Forces and the US Constitution itself do not allow the elevation or empowerment of one religious school of thought over any other, including the non-religious.

On the second assertion, however, and consistent with the line of reasoning herein presented, it is entirely possible to function and relate in a society from values that are generally humanistic or ethical and that overlap with the theology or belief systems of a variety of religious communities and/or faith traditions without practicing sectarianism's greatest liability: favoritism and exclusion. Neither favoritism nor exclusivism are democratic or suggestive of equal standing under the law, which is foundational in a liberal constitutional society (in the form the United States happens to be).

Protestant reformers of sixteenth century Europe claimed that vocation, beyond religious orders, was everyone's call from God for service in and across the communities of this world. Thus, as previously claimed, regarding public education as a "sacred calling" need not imply a specifically religious or sectarian orientation or purpose with regard to the shaping of education policy or practice.

For those who may be interested, appendix A offers a biblical rationale that, if extended two millennia, still is relevant and, one can say, justifies and prompts public policy advocacy and intentional citizen involvement from a nonsectarian, faith-values perspective for the common good. This, arguably, can include citizen involvement in an enterprise such as public education and its manifestations in the United States (and those not interested in a biblical rationale, of course, can skip this part).

---

1. White, "Intolerance Found at Air Force Academy"; Lisee, "Air Force Academy: Proselytizing and Religious Freedom Debate on School Campus."

The purpose and scope of this book is to present, to use a somewhat antiquated term, a primer. A primer is a small book that serves as an introduction to basics. A spelling primer, for example, would teach the alphabet and simple word constructions with consonants, vowels, and dictionary-like examples and illustrations. A primer in mathematics would teach addition, subtraction, and multiplication tables.

A primer related to public education identifies histories and evolution, challenges and assets, goals and approaches, and contextual diversities and similarities. The primer functions to orient beginners—if you will—to the core material of the subject. For this reason, there is no attempt to be comprehensive and exhaustive, no assertion made that this presentation is comprehensive and exhaustive, nor any implication that the conclusions are completely objective and nonpartisan.

This primer's angles and arguments flow and follow from a particular three-point thesis: (1) That public education is the moral and ethical—as well as the institutional—responsibility of a Western democracy like the United States; (2) that such an endeavor can thrive only with very broad and deep support from large, critical-mass numbers of citizen-stakeholders; and (3) that nonsectarian faith communities have philosophical and theological foundations and underpinnings that can create involved support to supplement and augment the institution and enterprise that is public education and can do so without compromising or violating the stipulations of the US Constitution's First Amendment.

A primer of this kind can be helpful for all stakeholders, especially those desiring a broader view and introduction to what others face and to what others have experienced, observed, argued, and learned. While not intending to exclude education professionals, among the individuals who might potentially find the content of this primer engaging are school board members, university students who are education majors, parents of students, and other citizen supporters (stakeholders) of public education.

Additionally, it is my hope in this effort that, after perusing these pages, citizens of various faith traditions might feel prompted to give informed support and consistent participation to public education, generally and specifically; and I hope that those who are not involved or interested in a tradition or community of faith might consider how faith-tradition adherents who are not sectarian in their beliefs and practices can be partners with them for enhancing public education and the common good.

Finally, I would add that, while many citizen stakeholders are not specialists in public education, none are disqualified from participation in this immense effort. Certainly there are limitations implied by a lack of specialized training in education, but perhaps this qualifies those of us who are not specialists to make contributions that, at a minimum, fall into the classification of "an outside set of eyes," which is an essential part of all collaborative efforts. While there is absolutely nothing wrong with being a specialist, many, if not most of us, including specialists, can benefit from a broader (forest-level) and supplemental perspective in addition to the particular (tree-level) perspectives, roles, and tasks for which we are respectively trained, often engaged, and sometimes employed.

In the mid-twentieth century, process philosopher Charles Hartshorne wrote of this possibility: "Human beings are almost too close to themselves to be able to think honestly [and perhaps accurately?] about themselves."[2]

If Hartshorne was convinced of this in relation to the general human condition, I rationalize it as potentially legitimizing an effort of this type, if carefully undertaken by any and all of us.

---

2. As quoted in Peters, *The Creative Advance*, 142.

Chapter 4

Mentioning "The Main Thing" and "There Are No Do-Overs"

ONE OF STEPHEN COVEY's most memorable aphorisms for posi-tive life outcomes is, "The main thing is to keep the main thing the main thing."[1] Obviously, this pertains to focusing on a primary goal in order to move toward that goal with the highest degree of success possible at the time. Conceivably, an individual or group can improve (or have given periods of greater success) at keeping the main thing in view and in mind. An individual or group can also slip or become distracted, lose focus, and end up off-course with less than satisfactory outcomes.

Maintaining or losing focus is crucial, because, in the words of another aphorism, "There are no do-overs." Let's explore the second aphorism of this chapter's title first, and then explore the first half of the title in the next chapter.

Time, which becomes history, is experienced as the near fu-ture materializes and immediately begins, passing across the stage of the present moment by moment in succession, moving from one wing of the stage to the other. Reality has no reverse gear or rewind button. This is not to say that remediation, rehabilitation,

1. Covey, *The Seven Habits of Highly Effective People*.

transformation, healing, and even success are impossible in both the march of days and the "no do-over" nature of history and life. Better outcomes are possible, yet any outcomes are always their own distinct, unique moments. No moment or time period exactly replicates another. No moments or time periods ever repeat or duplicate the past. Situations of past and present can be all too similar—hair-pullingly so, especially in the case of addictive and other forms of destructive behavior—yet every moment has its own components, context, character, and characters, whether the total of such components is judged more positively or more negatively.

In 1929, Alfred North Whitehead wrote, "In the conditions of modern life, the rule is absolute: The [human] race which does not value trained intelligence is doomed. Not all your heroism, not all your social charm, not all your wit, not all your victories on land or at sea, can move back the finger of fate. Today we maintain ourselves. Tomorrow science will have moved forward yet one more step, and there will be no appeal from the judgment which will then be pronounced on the uneducated."[2]

The past is past (or passed). Do the near future and the distant future have a chance to show improvement when compared to the past and present? Absolutely! Yet that improvement, when sought in an effort and enterprise such as public education, only occurs through constructive, collaborative, conscientious—even creative and courageous—efforts by citizen stakeholders in a democracy, such as the USA, when healthy, life-shaping, life-changing goals of individuals and institutions are deliberated and pursued. There's very, very little luck involved! Phrased another way: Improvement has a higher percentage of possibility to develop to the extent that all concerned are able to keep the main thing the main thing, fully understanding how there are no do-overs.

This approach has two implications. First, since the best of the past cannot be cloned, duplicated, or reconstructed in either the near or the distant future, whether we like it or not, it is therefore essential to resist the temptation to wish for repeated good

---

2. Whitehead, *The Aims of Education and Other Essays*, 14.

results or improvements. As someone has observed: "Saying 'if only such-and-such' actually wastes valuable time!'"

"If only" is a pairing of words expressing neither a healthy root system nor a healthy above-ground system for anyone's life situation.

We study the past, therefore, not for old recipes to be re-cooked in a new day, but (a) to avoid repetition of past events' neg-ative outcomes; and (b) to discover clues of elements that yielded constructive outcomes in previous contexts, and which, if adapted (not to be confused with adopted) in the mix of present contexts, might contribute positively to contemporary paradigms, practices, and multiple working relationships that comprise the life we know as public. For example, to think, say, or act in ways that implicitly or explicitly suggest or pursue an "if only" perspective wastes valu-able, irreplaceable time.

Two elements here present themselves: "if only" and "wasting valuable, irreplaceable time." Consider how persons and groups waste valuable, irreplaceable time when saying, thinking, or act-ing counter to whatever might be more productive. Wistfully (and naively or lazily), some, many, most, or all of us say, "If only we could experience today in public schools the best of what I expe-rienced in my growing up (or in my career) during the _____s! (fill in 1950, 1960, 1970, 1980, etc.)" This approach is deficient for so many reasons that it would be insulting to delineate even one or two. There's the alternative possibility of acting positively with eyes on both present and future, valuing the time we have, and, when necessary, acting with a sense of urgency.

After three interviews with urban and suburban public school educators in the upper Midwest, when we were about to disperse, a follow-up conversation occurred on the parking lot of the church where we had met. Each of the three, plus the two pas-tors with them, acknowledged that after their children completed grade four in that city, all five adults transferred their children to non-public schools and did so with heavy consciences. Each of the five still devote energy and emotion to public education, three being public school employees and the two pastors being public school advocates. Yet all five expressed a realization that they had "a thirteen-year window" for the primary and secondary education of their children. They each felt ethically compelled to make such difficult decisions and moves because critical systemic changes and improvement would not and could not occur fast enough for their children to benefit directly.

Rather than saying, "If only" and wasting valuable and irrecoverable time, we can ask (and we do better when we ask): "What elements now in the past contributed to creating positive experiences in public education during such earlier times and contexts— whenever that might have been—and still have traction and relevance in today's contexts?"

Before advancing a list of positive characteristics in response to the previously asked question, as we seek an enhanced public education journey together, a review of the distinction between past and present is essential. Diane Ravitch writes:

> Those who claim our schools have deteriorated refer to a long lost time when public schools were segregated, excluded most students with disabilities, and had relatively few non-English-speaking students. It was also a time when teachers had near-complete authority in their classrooms. Anyone with a sense of history should admire the resilience of the engine of democracy, which has surmounted a political obstacle course over the past half-century . . . A vigorous debate about curriculum, pedagogy, and discipline should give rise to a curriculum reform movement and to efforts to restore teachers' autonomy and authority, not to a movement to privatize and deprofessionalize American public education. Today's "reformers" ought to know that even in the 1950s . . . critics warned that "Johnny couldn't read" and . . . that the schools' lack of rigor was causing the nation to fall behind the international competition.[3]

In 2015, a statistical analysis of Texas public schools verified, with current numbers, much of what Ravitch had described five years earlier. For example, in a twenty-year period from 1995 to

3. Ravitch, *The Death and Life of The Great American School System*, 253–54.

2015, the Texas public school population increased from 3.7 million to 5.1 million (39.9 percent). The number of students from low-income households increased from 1.7 million to 3.1 million (81.9 percent). The number of students who are not classified as being from economically disadvantaged homes has increased since 1995 from 1.93 million to only 2.0 million. Ethnically, the population within Texas public schools has changed from 1995 to 2015 in the following way: Anglos, 47 percent to 29.4 percent; Hispanics, 36 percent to 51.8 percent; African American, 14 percent to 12.7 percent; Asian, in 1995 not differentiated to 3.7 percent.[4]

Now we consider the question of what education characteristics were experienced in the past that were judged positive and helpful then and that might be positive and helpful in the present. Responses may include, yet not be limited to: (1) people supporting people; (2) tenacious teachers and administrators; (3) peers who offer encouragement; (4) affirmation and respect received from various persons; (5) an interested and invested public; (6) persons exemplifying kindness, conscientiousness, discipline, cooperation; (7) intellect- and skill-stimulating curricula; (8) valuing creativity, uniqueness, teamwork, and problem solving; (9) consideration of each individual's and each group's positive potential; (10) persons willing to share one another's burdens, nurture one another's dreams, and endorse adaptations when another's goals need adjusting; (11) participation as groups and communities in outreach and service opportunities; (12) leadership development and team-spirit enhancement; (13) mutuality in goals embraced and pursued; (14) accountability in personal and corporate relationships (related to family, peers, community, and professional groups) and accountability to goals (general and specific, articulated expressly and understood implicitly).

Even after a list of positive experiences and memories is elicited and cataloged, respective past and present contexts must be evaluated, asking if past and present elements have any similarity or congruence. Perhaps considering past contexts that yielded positive outcomes will contribute to the creation and experience of

4. Ramsey, "Analysis: Schools Changing, and Not How You Might Think."

positive outcomes in the near and distant future. Such a possibility is more likely when history and historical contexts and factors are accurately included to frame our evaluations, as Diane Ravitch has crucially demonstrated.[5]

Robert Putnam concludes his substantial volume, *Bowling Alone: The Collapse and Revival of American Community Life*, with a metaphorical admonition about community-building that seeks the development of "social capital" through "picnics" (or similar and related types of events and activities).[6] Putnam is certainly not literally advocating having picnics rise to the level of formalized institutional practice, yet he is hoping for and encouraging the practice of community and relationship-building to become, in many forms, an evolving, intentional set of action-and-relationship engagements that enhances social capital, and, we may say, enhances the "accrual and investment" of that social capital.

My own take on evaluations for current applicability and usefulness of past institutional (or personal) practices is not based on or taken from respective institutions' existence or from their previous practices, quantitative longevity, historical form, nostalgic appeal, or programmatic functioning, "organizationally speaking." Evaluations for current applicability and usefulness are, rather, based on or taken from past quantitative and qualitative results, from which we seek, in process, potential manifestations in the present with the potential for positive quantitative and qualitative outcomes that advance the main thing. In other words, I do not think Robert Putnam expects us all literally and mindlessly to take up picnicking. If his critique, though, is that increases in cultural encouragements for unfettered individualism—whether sloth-slow or cheetah-fast—undermine the crucial viability of important "giving-back" institutions— such as public education—then perhaps public education, as an enterprise across the entire nation, needs evaluating in terms of how well social capital is nurtured and developed.

Three years after Putnam published *Bowling Alone*, he published, with Lewis Feldstein, in 2003, *Better Together: Restoring*

5. Ravitch, *Death and Life*, 253–54.
6. Putnam, *Bowling Alone*, 414.

the American Community, in which they distinguish, in the "social capital processes, between "bonding social capital" (which links persons and groups who have much in common) and "bridging social capital" (which links persons and groups who have little in common). They characterize bonding as being easier and bridging as being substantially more difficult.[7]

The goals in educational or other institutions should never be employed or contorted to create a morass of quantitatively related daydreams ("pie in the sky") or pressures (a hell of anxiety in mind and body for so many). The goals here (as related to public education) should, rather, leave room for communities' respective adaptations and for encouraging excellence and creativity, with the expectation that varied new institutional forms and functions will, over time, manifest positive outcomes in the ever-valuable emerging present, because capacities for growing both bonding and bridging social capital have developed among us.

In the realms of both public and education, history and research (and even philosophy) are never our magic formulas, nor are they our electric prods; but history and research (and even philosophy) are our friends and teachers. Perhaps a worthy goal is the common good, which will include, in Putnam's words, striving for increased "social capital," both through bonding and through bridging.

Precisely because there are no do-overs, we must be diligent in keeping the main thing as the main thing, realizing how this effort, with such a goal, is accomplishable in the long term only to the extent that we understand how the main thing is never a fixed target.

---

7. Putnam and Feldstein, *Better Together*, 279.

Chapter 5

"Public" Is the Main Thing

NOW THAT WE'VE BRIEFLY explored the second half of the previous chapter's title ("There are no do-overs."), let's return to and examine at some depth the first half of that chapter's title, which refers to the main thing.

The main thing is "public." A healthy public nurtures individuals; yet individualism erodes and diminishes the health and vitality both of "public" and of all individuals who comprise the several communities of "public."

It's an often told story that, during the Constitutional Convention of 1787, in Philadelphia, following contentious, crucial, closed-door deliberation, as the delegates departed for the day, a resident of the city asked Benjamin Franklin: "Doctor, what have we got, a republic or a monarchy?" Rather than limiting his response to one of her two options, Franklin replied, adding a challenge: "A republic, Madam, if you can keep it."

Thus that document, in its prologue, includes such lofty goals and responsibilities as: "establish[ing] justice; provid[ing] for the common defense; promot[ing] the general welfare; and secur[ing] the blessings of liberty to ourselves and our posterity."

Some secularists and some sectarian religionists—for different reasons—may well object to this book's title and premise: Public education is a sacred calling. The secularists may object to any term with religious sources or connections when associated with a nonsectarian subject and enterprise, as public education is (at its best). Certain nonsectarian religious persons at times also join the secularists in this argument, suspicious that a term like "sacred" is best kept in one's (private) religious life, unmixed with public terminology and practices. Their perspective may be a sort of purist or separatist nonsectarianism. The sectarian religious person may object to this book's thesis because public education is (at its best) a nonsectarian endeavor, and how could that possibly (and legitimately) justify any association with an adjective like "sacred"?

It is my hope that secularists, nonsectarian purists among religious folk, and even sectarian religious persons might loosen their respective ideological belts enough to join others in supporting, rebuilding, reforming, and reestablishing public education as the priority of the republic, which it needs to be if it is to continue with health, vitality, and integrity. This hope is, I confess, however, maintained with no fantasy expectations. We should fully understand that some (or many) have so intellectually accepted what they judge to be irredeemable shortcomings in the philosophy, rationale, and conditions of public or common education that they have intellectually and emotionally accepted the opposite: the absolute need for education outside the public realm, either through independent schools or with home schooling settings and support systems.

Charles Leslie Green Jr., in *The Myth of the Common School*, argues persuasively that public education can only be revitalized through a relinquishment of efforts to teach according to values, since there is never assurance that common values have staying power. For this reason, "choice" in education must be a publicly advocated option.[1]

I would not disagree with Green's assessment about parents having a right and privilege to teach values to their daughters and

---

1. Green, *The Myth of the Common School*, x–xi, 278–88.

sons, an undertaking that a public institution has neither the privilege nor the ability to do thoroughly.

John Taylor Gatto has also argued against public education for reasons similar to Green, but more acerbically, convinced as he is that Horace Mann's nineteenth-century vision of public education—which would inculcate "United States' moral and civic values"—never held water, and even if it did, only its abandonment will yield education as needed. The education we need, Gatto believes, is based in New England ("Congregationalist") individualism and intellectual freedom, which cannot be handed over to the state, because the state, with its educational apparatus, will assume a role that is citizen-shaping in nature. That role, option, and responsibility, argues Gatto, appropriately abides within the citizenry and the most basic sub-groups, such as households and voluntary associations.[2]

While Green and Gatto are persuasive for many persons with their particular assessments and convictions, for the purpose of my argument, distinct from theirs, individual freedom and choice are elemental and basic, yet public institutions and personal engagement for a broad common good are to be considered as equally valuable and even essential for a democratic republic and a republican form of democracy, such as the one we have inherited and of which we are stewards.

In the words of Diane Ravitch: "(Public schools) are a primary mechanism through which a democratic society gives its citizens the opportunity to attain literacy and social mobility."[3]

Neil Postman's similar consideration is, "My faith is that . . . public school will endure since no one has created a better way to create a public . . ."[4]

To paraphrase Dr. Franklin: "You have been given public education, if you can keep it." Mindful that our focus in this chapter is the public as the main thing, let's explore—like a honeybee

---

2. Gatto, *Dumbing Us Down*, 73–94; Gatto, *The Underground History of American Education*, 132–45.

3. Ravitch, *Death and Life*, 6.

4. Postman, *The End of Education*, 196–97.

among the flowers in a garden—a few crucial thoughts of a few crucial thinkers.

The main thing is public. This main thing is not something requiring the capitulation or the extermination of the individual; yet there is a need for citizens and the public to curb and discipline the excesses of philosophical, political, and sociological individualism. How might this happen? Certainly an argument can be developed along binary, polarized, win-lose, right-wrong lines; and more nuanced debates can occur, less stereotypically from clearly opposite positions that are, nevertheless, intense and opinionated.

As an illustration, two giants in twentieth-century academic circles like John Dewey and John Rawls, separately wrote and taught on the subjects of education in theory and practice (Dewey) and "public" as the essential seedbed of a liberal democracy (Rawls). Even so, the concept of public education can never reflect an easy or natural marriage of the two. Dewey is a pragmatist who is convinced that education is a means to the end of being fully human, and democracy is a qualitative derivative of productive inquiry and education. Rawls is a political theorist who is convinced that citizens—with their varied resources—have an unending responsibility to provide for the common good, which includes the essential component of equitable educational opportunities.[5]

Orlando Patterson, in *Freedom: Volume 1, Freedom in the Making of Western Culture*, traces freedom as a dynamic idea and force from the practice of slavery and, later, serfdom. He argues how, across the centuries from ancient times, the tension and conflict among masters, slaves, and "non-mastery non-slaves" have incubated, birthed, sustained, and regenerated the dream about, the efforts for, and the practice of freedom. This development is no straight line of progress, but involves continual tension and conflict.[6]

Tracing the back-and-forth, up-and-down nature of this slavery-freedom struggle while probing economic, social, political, and even military elements, Patterson categorizes freedom's

5. Weber, "Dewey and Rawls on Education," in *Springer Science and Business Media B.V.* (31:361–82).

6. Patterson, *Freedom* Vol..I, xiii.

"still-birth," construction, universalization, institutionalization, and reconstruction. The sources and originating points that he identifies and explores to develop his thesis are more ancient than many post-Enlightenment moderns (at least those of us who are non-specialists) might suspect. As part of his conclusion, he writes:

> At best, the valorization of personal liberty is the noblest achievement of Western civilization. That people are free to do as they please within limits set only by the personal freedom of others; that legally all persons are equal before the law; that philosophically the individual's separate existence is inviolable . . . all add up to a value-complex . . . superior to any other single complex of values conceived by humankind . . . (Yet) At its worst, no value [i.e., personal freedom] has been more evil and socially corrosive in its consequences, inducing selfishness, alienation, the celebration of greed, and the de-humanizing disregard for the "losers," the "little people" who fail to make it . . .[7]

Why this seemingly extended excursus into philosophy, history, sociology, economics, and so forth, when the main thing is "public"? Because the most unrelenting opponents of "public" develop their arguments and feed their rationales on a diet of unexamined ideology that claims unqualified individual freedom (and free choice) as its life-line. If Patterson is on target, those who wish to abandon—and have freedom from the complexities of —"public" are, in the name of freedom, strategically, tactically, and humanly speeding into a curve with little accurate comprehension of the approaching consequences, certainly long-term, if not also short-term.

Rawls, in *Political Liberalism*, argues that "the good of a political society" is experienced as and when "citizens realize [justice as fairness], both as persons and as a corporate body, [through] maintaining a just constitutional regime and in conducting its affairs." He further writes: "A well-ordered society . . . is not, then, a private society; for, in the well-ordered society of justice as fairness, citizens do have final ends in common . . . They do not affirm

7. Ibid., 402–3.

the same comprehensive doctrine, (but) they do affirm the same political conception of justice."[8] (But do we "affirm the same political conception of justice" in real contexts?)

Rawls continues: "Political society is good for citizens" due to how "it secures for them the good of justice and the social bases of their mutual self-respect." Here Rawls presents the continual political and philosophical challenge: "The path justice as fairness must follow [is] to gain the support of an overlapping consensus [politically]." This necessity undercuts and/or transcends any "comprehensive religious, philosophical, or moral doctrine" that would include sectarian, nonsectarian, libertarian, or communitarian doctrines. "The priority of 'right' [justice as fairness] . . . must use political ideas . . . imposed by the political conception of justice . . ."[9]

Finally, Rawls asserts: "The definitive idea for deliberative democracy is the idea of deliberation itself." And, "Public deliberation must be recognized as a basic feature of democracy, and set free from the curse of money . . . [seeking] widespread education in the basic aspects of constitutional democratic government for all citizens . . . [who are] informed about pressing problems [in order to make] crucial political and social decisions."[10]

Robert Putnam points to a worrisome development and a serious crack in the foundation of "public," which would include Rawls's "justice as fairness." He writes, "Those who care about both liberty and community face a painful trade-off."[11] Putnam then quotes Michael Schudson: "The decline in organizational solidarity [in the 1980s and 1990s] is truly a loss, but is also the flip side of a rise in individual freedom, which is truly a gain . . ."[12] At this point Putnam adds (somewhat cynically): "We (as two persons or

8. Rawls, *Political Liberalism*, 201, 202.

9. Ibid., 202, 203.

10. Ibid., 448, 449.

11. Putnam, *Bowling Alone*, 354.

12. Putnam, quoting Schudson, *The Good Citizen*, 307.

as two groups) no longer connect; but at least I don't bother you and you don't bother me."[13]

Then Putnam adds with clarity: "It is hard to imagine that we can meet the challenges . . . for America . . . without using government . . . What is needed to restore trust and community bonds in America is [both] individual change [and] institutional change." His afterword and acknowledgments begin with his characterization of his primary *Bowling Alone* thesis as relating to "a decline of generalized reciprocity—the practice of helping others with no expectation of gain."[14]

Obviously, one cannot naively or mindlessly link sets of sociological observations, noting Putnam's "decline of helping others with no expectation of gain," with Rawls's philosophical and political argument for "justice as fairness." Even so, both of these orbit the concept of "public," and do so with reverence.

With equal reverence, Alan Wolfe and Theda Skocpol sound warnings for "public" from their respective observations.

Wolfe, in *Moral Freedom: The Search for Virtue in a World of Choice*, writes how "Americans today . . . who support greater 'school choice' through vouchers and charter schools see freedom of choice as a way of encouraging greater [public school] institutional responsibility . . . Finding the balance between institutional authority and freedom will never be easy . . . Like alcohol, too much moral freedom can be a dangerous thing." Then he observes: "Once people are free to choose their cars and their candidates, they will not long be satisfied with letting others determine for them the best way to live. As correct as critics [conservative and liberal] of America's moral condition are to insist on the need for shared understandings of the moral life, it is better, given moral freedom's inevitability, to think of [this] as a challenge to be met, rather than as a condition to be cured."[15]

Skocpol, in *Diminished Democracy: From Membership to Management in America's Civic Life*, describes the paradox of first,

13. Putnam, *Bowling Alone*, 354.

14. Ibid., 413, 505.

15. Wolfe, *Moral Freedom*, 228–29, 230.

a United States' majority who desire social protection through positive government roles (law and order, civil rights, regulations against usurious and monopolistic practices, environmental and public health standards and oversight); and second, interest group efforts that oppose and stunt more comprehensive political and legislative efforts, including public education. She advocates the development of "new strategies for translocation association-building" that facilitate "for our own times . . . great voluntary combinations . . . for the vigorous practice of civil and political democracy."[16]

The authors quoted thus far during this chapter's "main thing" discussion related to "public" all wrote during the last thirty years of the twentieth century or the first decade of the twenty-first century. Let us, however, look to a volume written in 1952 by Walter Prescott Webb and to an essay written in 1953 by Isaiah Berlin for characterizations that conclude this chapter on "public" as the main thing.

In his book, *The Great Frontier*, Webb calls to mind three reflective, personally held beliefs by three different political leaders. First, from 1781, Thomas Jefferson of Virginia addresses the goal of schools from elementary grades to university learning, which is "to diffuse knowledge more generally through the mass of the people." Because the stewardship of good government is entrusted to that mass of people, "their minds must be improved to a certain degree." Second, from the 1840s, consider the words of Texas leader Sam Houston: "The benefits of education and of useful knowledge, generally diffused through a community, are essential to the preservation of a free government." Finally, Houston's Texas contemporary, Mirabeau Lamar, states: "A cultivated mind is the guardian genius of democracy . . . It is the only dictator that free [persons] acknowledge, and the only security which free [persons] desire."[17]

Berlin's essay articulated his understanding of the Russian literary giant, Leo Tolstoy and was titled, "The Hedgehog and the Fox." Berlin draws his primary metaphor from the ancient Greek, Archilochus, who wrote, "The fox knows many things, but the hedgehog

16. Skocpol, *Diminished Democracy*, 240–41, 292–93.
17. Webb, *The Great Frontier*, 394.

knows one big thing." Berlin believed that Tolstoy, by nature, was a fox, knowing many things, but that he evolved into hedgehog similarities through his "unifying vision" that history is comprised of many factors, many of which accumulate to influence succeeding elements, moments, persons, relationships, and events.[18]

Drawing from Berlin's method in assessing Tolstoy, one can observe how education as a subject and in its many varied forms and phases is certainly fox-like. If "public" is an invaluable asset, "public" might also be the organic concept-of-origin and nutrient-for-growth that serves as a democratic republic's potentially unifying vision and purpose. If this possibility evolves and develops in positive manifestations, we all may benefit by experiencing unimagined development in a direction that is more "hedgehogian" in terms of "public," while we remain adequately "foxian" in terms of education. A helpful "hedgehog" orientation certainly can make the case that the main thing is "public."

18. Berlin, "The Hedgehog and the Fox: An Essay on Tolstoy's View of History," in *The Proper Study of Mankind*, 436–98.

Chapter 6

Varied Education Trajectories

GIVEN THAT THERE ARE no do-overs and that it is crucial, even imperative, to keep the main thing the main thing, for the purposes of this primer it may be helpful to think of education—and public education in particular—as a type of competition, within the context of which falling behind very far creates serious consequences.

If one is competing in a contest of this nature, understanding the goals, strategies, plans, and skills involved in the competition is essential. Here is both the rub and the mountain to climb.

Consider this analogy: If engaged in orchestra competition, at the most basic level, playing the instruments adequately for the expected skill level of the competition is a goal for success. The same is true for marching bands and other fine arts, academic content mastery, business skills, or in science, technology, or athletic contests. For now, however, we'll stick with the orchestra analogy.

Once the basic essentials of instrumental and artistic competence are comprehended and mastered, one's task is only beginning. The goals, rules, and scoring criteria of the particular competitive endeavor must be learned. Then the potential strategies by which the goals can be reached should be identified, explored, learned, considered, and chosen. From a determined strategy, sequential plans for the competition itself can be charted and prioritized. When the competition begins, the plans are implemented through the time allowed, after which competition evaluations are finalized and announced, and planning for subsequent competition begins a new but similar cycle. At the end of a season or series of competitive events (or, occasionally, during the season), different strategies may be considered and adopted.

As we shall see related to education, over a period of years, even the goals may change, and the skills necessary for success may vary. This primer does not attempt to write a history of education or explore in-depth various and competing education theories and their implementation, nor does it attempt to survey numerous efforts at reform. If it is one's goal, however, to learn aspects of the complex game—or, better, the endeavor—that comprises education as an institution, I am most helped by the notion of working backwards. One may best begin with observations from lay-of-the-land results and then trace connecting elements backwards to the origins. Phrased differently, one may explore from effects back to causes.

Crime scene investigators, we are told, often use a method like this to determine the source-position of a shooter. Approximations are calculated on the supposed position of the victim and the angle of the bullet entry. These calculations suggest the likely trajectory of the bullet. While no one is being shot in the United States' various educational endeavors, investigating backward from the present can yield important considerations about the trajectory of the goals toward which communities, schools, and/or parents have their students aimed.

Returning to our beginning metaphor of orchestra competition, let us consider observations, research, and investigations of the current situation and lay of the land. If one knows little or nothing about orchestra competition, one might start by becoming acquainted with the rules and the scoring criteria. One might then evaluate one's own orchestra members' apparent talent. One might research each one's background and training, along with the origins and history of the musical arrangement they will be playing. One could estimate the strengths and weaknesses of the orchestra conductor and the chemistry among the musicians, the conductor, and the anticipated audience. One might explore the type and quality of the musicians' instruments and the acoustical capabilities of the performance venue where the competition will be presented. One could even include the adequacy or inadequacy of funding resources for the orchestra and participants. And lastly, after assessing one's own orchestra's capability factors, one might assess the competition's strengths and the contest judges' preferences and pet peeves.

Surely I've omitted one or more relevant factors. The point, though, is that positive results in orchestra competition do not happen by chance. Results always are first, a complex, composite sum and second, an algorithmic calculation with many more contributing factors than can be easily assessed, measured, or even taken into account.

Public education is no different, and the sooner we awaken to this reality, the better off all will be. Every day it's "game on" for success! What do we need to understand about the contest for the common good into which we are called as participants, even competitors, related to the educational enterprise?

Imagine observing (even celebrating) a class of students processing into an auditorium or outdoor venue, receiving diplomas and degrees, and recessing at a commencement exercise. What's the story behind them? What are the factors, interactions, and experiences that combined to yield this result? What set of family, school system, and cultural influences brought them along this trajectory from a few years before to the day of their graduation?

One can argue that, in the United States and possibly elsewhere, varied education trajectories culminating in graduation or receiving a diploma originate from a common method that, broadly, can be characterized as "means-to-ends." From initial enrollment in kindergarten classes to graduation from high school, students, their families, educators, and the school systems aim toward an end of success and graduation.

Looking backward from a goal like graduation, one rightly asks: "How can this be achieved? What plans—contemplated and implemented—get the student (and all of us) there?"

In and of itself, a means-to-ends method related to any aspect of life is hypothetically value-neutral. It's neither bad nor good as an idea, desire, or an analytical tool for what is done. In its implementation, however, we should presume that real circumstances yielding real results can and should be evaluated in practice for consistency and correspondence with positive goals and objectives.

To repeat my previously stated bias and conviction, the essential and positive conveyance of quality education in our United States democratic republic is necessarily supported by the public institutions of government and citizens. While we can agree that students' success leading to graduation is part of a crucial, common goal of every and all education efforts, the means to the end—what happens and how what occurs actually develops—are valued in this perspective according to norms at the heart of "public." These norms include, but are not limited to equitable opportunity for each and all, whole-community access to similar quality services, and consideration of both the present and the future as important for one and all.

How and what means—methods and resources—are employed, engaged, and appropriated daily make a difference in the quality and validity of the ends (outcomes) that individuals and groups hope to achieve.

For example, while we might agree that cheating is not an acceptable means to an end, and that an end accomplished by way of cheating is morally and ethically tarnished (if not illegitimate and invalid), we then often find ourselves in situations where we need to decide if it's better to work hard and long to accomplish a goal with more modest success, or even failure, than with the success that cheating could provide. This is worth considering far beyond the classroom where students are involved; thus the following example from another arena of "public."

On June 25, 2013, in Austin, Texas, a scenario developed toward the end of special session of the legislature. The State senate was debating a bill that would greatly increase regulations on certain women's health clinics in the state. The majority party held an 18–11 favorable margin in elected members, but toward the end of the debate, at about 11:45 p.m., just before the time of the legislative session would expire at midnight, the presiding officer (a member of the majority party) so manipulated the parliamentary rules that the packed crowd of citizens in the balcony seats lost patience and erupted into continuous yells of protest. The volume of noise was so loud and sustained that it inhibited and prevented the presiding officer from completing the vote that he and his party desired to conclude before that midnight deadline. This chaos occurred not simply because the crowd in the balcony opposed the bill that had the majority votes to pass. The chaos—and inability to act on the pending legislation—occurred because the senate's presiding officer and his majority colleagues judged that the end of winning their vote before midnight justified their over-the-top disregard of established rules of parliamentary fair play. To their frustration, however, the citizen-crowd noise impeded their intentions for just long enough. (Subsequently, during a special session of the legislature called to consider this issue that, in the majority party's opinion, was lacking satisfactory resolution, the women's health clinic restrictions were passed using recognized parliamentary rules.)

Means-to-ends methods (as trajectories, of sorts) are not value-neutral when employed in real-life situations. Their effect can be more or less positive, or more or less negative. In the next few pages, we shall survey how means-to-ends thinking and efforts influence and comprise numerous aspects of educational endeavors and create certain trajectories, beginning with types of schools.

Means-to-ends goals and efforts yield different types of schools with differently nuanced objectives and with different types of support resources. Broadly applied to United States education institutions, the general distinction within pre-kindergarten through grade 12 types of schools is whether the school is public or private (also known as independent). The classification distinction here can be based mostly upon the means, which is the funding type, applied toward the end or goal, which is education for all who show up in the classification of "public" and for those able to be admitted in the classification of "private" or "independent."

For public education, the means, then, of tax-generated revenues exists due to a public constituency and a constitutional democratic institutional system, which is understood by public education stakeholders as a morally and/or historically necessary commitment in order to provide the end: a quality education for each citizen. Different from private or independent education efforts that have limiting qualifying criteria, public education's single qualifying criterion is that every student is part of "the public." This may, in fact, be so radically inclusive that it is hardly possible to classify it as a qualifying criterion at all.

Public schools exist in different forms. Among these are area-specific schools, magnet schools, charter schools, select schools, and specialty schools. These five can generally be defined as follows.

Area-specific: Students attend from within specified geographic boundaries determined by a district board. Curriculum is usually basic and broad-based, even when specialty departments exist within such schools.

Magnet: Students choose to attend magnet schools due to specialty offerings and concentrations such as science and technology, mathematics, fine arts, foreign languages, etc. Magnet schools are not necessarily exclusive of all general studies' curricula; and magnet schools may also share building sites and facilities with an area-specific school. In such cases, the district's students who live outside the boundaries of the specific area for that school are encouraged to apply for admission to the magnet school if interested in the magnet course offerings.

Charter: These schools are established and administered outside of and different from traditional public schools. Charter schools meet standards—either State standards or local district standards—in order to receive their charter, essentially a license to operate in accordance with the requirements of the particular charter. Some are public charter schools and receive tax-based or even enhanced revenues when compared to their area-specific sibling schools. Others are founded, funded, and administered by foundations, parents and/or educators, or community groups. Charter schools may also feature: (a) non-union or off-state-payscale faculty and staff; (b) students who meet particular enrollment criteria; (c) substantial supplemental funding from private and corporate donors; and (d) curricula specialization, alternative education, and programs designed for differing learning methods and styles.[1]

Select: These schools are open to students who meet exceptionally narrow enrollment criteria. In urban school districts, qualifying for a select school is often a long-range and high-pressure goal for students and/or their parents. Testing success on entrance exams (or exams during previous school years) and personal interviews are usually part of the application process.

Specialty: These schools are similar to magnets since they also offer narrowly defined areas of concentration, yet they do so to the exclusion of general studies students from the neighborhood, who only attend select schools if selected based on the high admissions standards, in equal competition with those others who are admitted from beyond the neighborhood of the campus or school site.

Private or independent schools exist for the end or goal of high quality educational opportunities. Without public tax-based revenue, their financial means are generated from private sources such as students' families, alumni giving, and corporate or religious funding. Private or independent schools also exist in different forms. Some are secular in nature; others are religious. Some have specialty emphases. Some are characterized by "home schooling," where participants learn from instructors who are adult family members or arranged tutors, either on site or online. (The home school enterprise has grown exponentially since 1990 through entrepreneurial networks and communities that make

---

1. For a detailed account of charter school development, see Ravitch, *Death and Life*, 122–27.

possible learning resources, leadership development, and teacher support for home school leaders, both parents and tutors.)

The private, independent, and home-school endeavor is related to the argument for choice. As mentioned in chapter 3, citing Alan Wolfe's conclusions, proponents of this means-to-ends trajectory conclude that education—either short-term or long-term—yields more positive results for students who are engaged in private/independent opportunities than would be possible for them in public school systems and settings, at least for the present.

The historic "common good" emphasis and goal of public education may, at times, be a stated goal of private and independent education efforts, but the common good as related to public education is never enhanced directly from private and independent education institutions. It is true that private and independent education proponents periodically argue that an indirect enhancement for public education can result from market competition with private and independent alternatives. Competing enterprises and markets, they believe, enhance the product of both.

Such an argument, while possibly convincing to some by way of alleged common sense and real-life factors at a surface level, is seriously flawed. While private/independent education efforts and schools have every right to exist (and thrive) in a free society, and while competition, hypothetically, can be positive as a marketplace incentive in order for various systems to strive to produce a high quality product, private/independent education endeavors are exposed under the microscope each time evidence is revealed of substantial (even vast) inequitable per-student resource differences and of the ignoring of the foundational premise that each child in a society deserves equitable opportunities in personal development (an end or goal).

This equity of resources and provision of equitable opportunities is the essence of public priority and the responsibility of a public institution such as government (legislative, executive, and judicial; local, state and federal). For this reason, any legislation to create vouchers or tax benefits to households who would rather enroll their children in private/independent schools and be spared the expense of supporting public schools via public taxation, while understandable as being financially favorable for those households, can pose a serious threat to funding bases and public taxation for public schools.

Having briefly considered how varied education trajectories originate from means-to-ends methods and can lead to differing types of schools, we now consider how education trajectories from means-to-ends methods can yield multiple goals, objectives, and prioritized responsibilities (and please see appendix C for an outline chart of this discussion).

The six goals here listed do not represent a comprehensive and exhaustive inventory. They are selective, yet broad, include a variety of categories and elements, and are relevant both to public and private or independent education efforts and groups.

1. Meeting empirical standards. This is perhaps the most widely known and commonly debated priority that a survey might identify. Students are expected to perform at levels pre-determined for satisfactory grades on standardized tests, often associated with subject content and process mastery. Faculty are also often evaluated by their students' performances on such standardized tests, as are entire grades, classes, individual schools, local districts, state systems, and education participants and systems nationally. One of the more interesting evaluative questions addressing this particular goal, objective, and prioritized responsibility was raised by a group of Texas public school superintendents during the year 2008. In requesting a temporary waiver from federal "No Child Left Behind" test score standards (later, during the succeeding Obama administration, known as "Race to the Top"), the Texas superintendents argued that standards that judge entire classes of students and their respective schools were in need of reevaluation. If an individual or collective body needs to reach, let's say, a score of 70 to be determined satisfactory, how fair or positive is it to declare "satisfactory" the tested/evaluated individual/group that begins the year at 69 and concludes the year at 71, when a different individual/group begins the year at 58 and concludes the year at

68, but then is declared unsatisfactory and failed? Satisfying goals through meeting empirical performance proficiency standards is important. Yet using evaluative means and formulas that fail to allow for contingent contextual factors creates, perpetuates, and widens the gap between success and failure, between a sense of achievement and a sense of defeat. In the words of the Texas superintendents' recommendations, "Standards should be framed so they do not sacrifice the profound learning [that is] desired for easy and low-cost state assessment and accountability measures."[2]

2. Equipping students. While it is essential, additionally, to equip faculty, support staff, administrators, parents/families, and other constituents, a primary goal, objective, and prioritized responsibility continually at the heart of both public and private/independent education is equipping students. This is variously articulated and desired. Related to the empirical standards mentioned above, students are being equipped for meeting such standards as measured by testing or other evaluative forms. Somewhat differently and more broadly, classical liberal education traditionally has sought to equip students for far more than success on standardized content-mastery tests. In all subjects, from math and science to social studies and languages, from kindergarten through grade 12, problem solving, in-depth reasoning skills, artistic and rhetorical expression, relationship building, social sciences, political, historical, philosophical, and literary analysis, and other disciplines are emphasized to equip students for citizenship in a world that needs each one to be broadly equipped in both sciences and humanities for the best public, relational, and evolving implications in ongoing, changing contexts.[3] Alfred North Whitehead argued for this point of view as early as 1917: "The antithesis between a technical and a liberal education is fallacious. There can be no adequate

2. See Texas Association of School Administrators, "Creating a New Vision for Public Education in Texas," 14.

3. See Ayers, *To Teach*, 103–6; and Barzun, *Teacher in America*, 314–16.

technical education which is not liberal, and no liberal education which is not technical."[4]

3. Facilitating change. This goal, objective, or prioritized responsibility can and does relate to evolutionary realities recognized by leaders in education policy and practice. Even devotees of content/ process-mastery and of satisfying empirical standards often recognize that facilitating change is a positive element in desirable curricular outcomes. This component of longer trajectories may be understood in two ways: more particularly, as in assisting students, by way of their curricula, to cope with forecast changes through the stages and varying situations that they will face across the years; and more generally, as in assisting students, by way of their curricula, to engage with the persons and institutions comprising regional and global constituencies for adapting and building toward ends that relate to the sciences, to the arts and humanities, and to cultures and civilizations. At its best, this is never change for change's sake, but involves change for the common good in multiple and often complex ways.

4. Engaging and being engaged by the community, the public, or the support base. This goal, objective, or prioritized responsibility clearly indicates the relationships of all education endeavors, enterprises, and institutional forms to a wider community and cultures. When persons are, beyond the day-to-day internals of schools and education systems, informed, energized, motivated, oriented, and connected with varied aspects of schools' and students' educational, institutional, and individual needs, the whole of the enterprise can be strengthened. This occurs in areas of funding, learning, energy, morale, alliance-building, legislation-facilitating, and more. Perhaps no one articulates this need and goal better than David Mathews in *Reclaiming Public Education by Reclaiming Our Democracy*.[5]

---

4. Whitehead, "Technical Education and Its Relation to Science and Literature" in *The Aims of Education and other Essays*, 43–59.

5. Mathews, *Reclaiming Public Education by Reclaiming Our Democracy*, 8, 14, 17–18.

5. Creating institutional recognition or reputation and political and economic gravitas and leverage. These two goals, objectives, and prioritized responsibilities relate to positive reputations and getting one's brand out there so that support develops and grows through public, political, economic, and governmental institutions and entities and, additionally, through private households, businesses, industry, not-for-profits, and others. (The standards and metrics for progress and success in these areas can be observed through the degrees of quantity and quality related to #4.)

6. Enhancing ideological magnetism and appeal. If #5 focuses on strong, positive reputations with already sympathetic supporters (both individuals and corporate entities), this goal, objective, and prioritized responsibility seeks to develop converts and new supporters from those previously unengaged. Who might share the vision of the school, the district, the larger alliance or enterprise that currently is not engaged in supportive roles of varying types and capacities? As noted with the previous five goals, objectives, and prioritized responsibilities, this sixth need relates to both public and private/independent education endeavors. Any vision of particular educational entities or alliances may vary from one to another. Moreover, schools of the same type—whether public or private/independent—may market their particular vision by way of messaging that explicitly or implicitly promotes the benefits of their educational program and possible results.

Mathews is convinced that the most effective challenge-responses and results enhancements associated with public education occur through engagement that is "citizen-to-citizen before it can be citizen-to-school or school-to-community."[6]

This chapter's extended assessment of numerous, often complex elemental factors and directions related to education—and the competition to keep up in relation to achievement and resources—has explored identifiable trajectories originating out of

---

6. Ibid., 78.

means-to-end methods. We now shift, in the following chapter, to assessing varied education approach-perspectives.

These approach-perspectives become evident as they are employed, first, in relation to perceived (and selected) challenges and reactions; and second, in relation to the identification of arguable elements and context dynamics, toward which strategies, tactics, and efforts are developed and exercised in the quest for achieving desired goals.

Chapter 7

Approach-Perspectives to Twelve Challenge Topics

REMEMBER OUR PREVIOUS ANALOGY: positive results in orchestra competition do not happen by chance. Results always are a complex composite sum and an algorithmic calculation with many more contributing factors than can be easily assessed, measured, or even taken into account. Education, including public education, is no different, and the sooner we awaken to this reality, the better off all will be. Every day it's "game on" for success! What do we need to understand about the contest for the common good into which we are called as participants, even competitors, related to the education enterprise or endeavor?

In the previous chapter we explored means-to-ends trajectories that first, weight formation and typology decisions as schools originate, develop, and seek to fulfill federal and state acceptable standards; and that second, shape goals, objectives, and prioritized responsibilities for positive outcomes within various districts and schools.

Here we shall explore means-to-ends approach-perspectives when perceived challenges and responses/reactions move and shake within education contexts. (Subsequently we shall explore arguable elements and context dynamics that are identified as debate-worthy for the common good, along with some particular components or side effects judged presently to be in play, when considering the common good.)

Imagine that we have an interpretive lens for examining and assessing the appropriateness and adequacy of competitive elements among varied education entities. Using it, a person might observe numerous elements within respective education endeavors, which are sometimes different only by degree and nuance and which are sometimes quite different in substance, method, strategy, and tactics.

Returning to the orchestra analogy, different types of music (classical, military march, jazz, folk, country, blues, etc.) feature and emphasize different respective instruments and different styles of playing. Also, a particular musical selection or composition may evoke different interpretive emphases by different conductors as they plan and rehearse for a performance. Other fine arts, athletics, and academic competitions can be analyzed similarly, because all follow certain rules for competition, and all follow certain norms and typologies to develop strategies and tactics in relation to available talent, along with how opposing contestants and factors might blend and create challenges during the competition itself.

Education approach-perspectives may be explored and analyzed by identifying angles and aspects that leader-participants judge to be crucial. If accepting a premise that a person or group operates (and competes) from a given value or set of values, that person or group will sense challenges to those values and then often will react or respond with methods and means that attempt either to maintain or to extend the prioritized values or set of values that are being challenged.

Let's now attempt to enhance our understanding of the competitiveness (even contentiousness) within education efforts, and to do so, first, through examining challenges related to twelve priority topics, values, and subject areas that education leaders and education-related entities/institutions feel led to nurture, to defend, or to strengthen.

Before rolling out these twelve challenges and approach-perspective responses or reactions and the eleven questions in the next chapter related to public education for the common good, let's be clear why developing an analytical dexterity of this type is important: If you can identify the means employed and/or the value and priority being defended or advanced, cleaner judgments can be made about the validity of that rationale and approach, given one's own values and priorities.

Phrased differently, and returning to the orchestral performance metaphor, what if a musician who is reading sheet music cannot recognize a rest symbol? Even if all notes are played flawlessly, there's no way for the musician to play the music as the composer intended or as the conductor desires, in order to create a coordinated effort with other musicians who are reading the rests correctly. By contrast, flawless note performance with recognition and incorporation of rest symbols can yield a coordinated orchestral effort.

Similarly, if theory, policy, or implementation arguments are being advanced by someone, even someone with impressive credentials and recognized expertise, when a listener (however inexperienced) can analyze the argument contents and the often unmentioned implications, then the listener is equipped to be a capable contributor both to the debate and to a given situation's potential constructive next steps and even enhancement.

As citizen stakeholders, not one of us is called or required to be an expert in all areas. Both orchestral performance and education theories and systems, with cultural factors that are both subtle and overt, are complex in the extreme. We are not required to be experts in all areas. A broad awareness of the varied and diverse elements and issues that comprise the challenges we face, however, enhances each individual's skills, appreciation, and confidence for participation as a citizen stakeholder in this immense challenge and supremely important endeavor.

Now, consider the list in this chapter of twelve approach-perspectives related to perceived challenges and responses or reactions (with the goal of enhancing our pursuit of "public education for the common good").

Think of essentials, of basics, and of highly desired outcomes. Each person (and each one of innumerable groups) represents particular opinions, outlooks, and values related to multiple factors in life, education, and citizenship. Central to this angle of analyzing education is the simple inquiry seeking to identify what desire or purposes a debate or policy is attempting to address in order to nurture, to defend, or to strengthen the particular desire or purpose.

Such actual challenges may be dreams or undesired deficiencies. They may be candidly named because the pursuers both of accomplishment and of remedy sincerely believe these are the actual challenges important to address. Other actual challenges may lie behind the curtain of what is named as the challenge in a conversation, a memo, or a debate. Discerning the difference is crucial. Then one must determine whether or to what degree proposed solutions or counter-measures are agreed with or not agreed with, what compromises are possible, and what alternatives need to be pursued (please see appendix D for an outline chart of this content).

1. When the challenge named is "results" . . . Particular challenges may arise or be anticipated that lead to reactions or responses focused around results. The desired results may be measured from scores on content-mastery tests and/or skill-proficiency-demonstration exams. The individuals engaged for standardized achievement or improved results may be individual students, entire class grades, entire schools, entire districts, states, or the nation. Classroom educators and school administrators may then be judged by students' success or failure on their scores.

2. When the challenge named is "context" . . . Particular challenges may arise, or be anticipated, that lead to reactions or responses focused around contexts. Of course, contexts vary from urban to suburban, to small city, town, or rural, from mostly healthy individuals, homes, neighborhoods, schools, and school districts

to dysfunctional, under-resourced, and discouraged individuals, homes, neighborhoods, schools, and school districts. While all challenges have a context, this challenge classification, when in need of a means-to-end action plan for improvement, is exemplified—as one example among innumerable examples—where there exists a substantial shortage of accredited classroom teachers. A response or reaction decision may be made by a school district to contract or partner with an organization such as Teach for America (TFA). While a decision of this nature provides no long-term solution to the particular district, Teach for America certainly may be able to assist in providing an immediate or intermediate fix, given such a contextual challenge.[1]

3. When the challenge named is "cost" . . . Particular challenges may arise, or be anticipated, that lead to reactions or responses focused around cost. The commonly understood subject here is financial in nature, as related to income and expenses, tax assessments and tax revenues, capital assets, payroll, property, and utilities, plus individual and corporate donations. Additional cost challenges to the larger equation are, at times, related to such subjects as performance standards, graduation rates, average daily attendance, etc. The corporate, group, and community stress associated with performance standards, graduation rates, average daily attendance, and potential penalties when the mandated minimum success levels are not met, creates an emotional cost among students, faculty, administrators, and the broader community. Additionally, cost cutting that reduces faculty, courses offered, education services (primary or auxiliary), student and family support assistance, and other services can create collateral costs and expenses among those individuals and households affected, as well as for the particular school district. Lowered morale in the lives of all who are affected, both directly and indirectly, often figures among the emotional and collateral expenses of extreme cost cuts.

4. When the challenge named is "faith" . . . Particular challenges may arise, or be anticipated, that lead to reactions or responses focused

---

1. Farr, Kopp, and Kamras, *Teaching As Leadership*, 216–17, 235.

around faith. While faith-based institutions such as churches have been engaged in the school business longer than public education has been widespread, a discussion of faith as part of public education may seem out of place or even out of order. Challenges, however, still arise within classrooms, schools, districts, and states regarding practices, content, theory, and policy that spring from religious values of various types. The challenge advocates may be persons or groups proposing the exercise or expression of particular faith-traditions or religions. The challenge advocate may be a person seeking a tolerant, safe refuge from one or more others who desire to bring faith-practices into public and nonsectarian settings. Particular subject areas in this category may be (but are not limited to) textbook selection, curricula adoption, spoken prayer, extracurricular Bible study groups, and others. With the US Constitution's First Amendment prohibiting any establishment of religion, an entity and institution such as public education is duty-bound to safeguard—through policy and in practice—a nonsectarian and neutral, non-advocacy approach-perspective (means) toward every end or goal pursued or undertaken that would cross the safeguard line for every person who does not wish to feel even slightly uncomfortable. A public school or system should not become a venue or cell site for even a potentially expanded sphere sought by any religious person or group. (This is easier written and said than it is accomplished.)

5. When the challenge named is "requirements" . . . Particular challenges may arise, or be anticipated, that lead to reactions or responses focused around requirements. Such requirements decided and enacted by governing bodies or administrative personnel often have financial implications, employee and staff implications, building implications, academic implications, and attendance implications, and the bearers of responsibility may be the citizen stakeholders, governing entities, administrators, educators, students, or parents. While any particular person or group may feel irritated in relation to requirements, without appropriate requirements with equitable standards—for employee certification, for student achievement, for proficiency, for curricula, for basic

financing, for attendance, for inclusiveness and special needs—
then crucial aspects of the public education endeavor or enterprise
are more easily ignored or left underachieved, to the detriment of
students and faculty. The end goal of requirements frequently—
yet not always—sets important standards for the means that make
possible positive ends. The crucial factor is that requirements are
appropriate and extend through their enactment toward integra-
tive results that further equity and the common good within and
across communities.

6. When the challenge named is "needs" . . . Particular challenges
may arise, or be anticipated, that lead to reactions or responses
focused around needs. Needs differ from requirements in that requirements are imposed by a higher authority. Needs are part of
challenges recognized by those in one segment of a group. Superintendents, principals, counselors, custodial personnel, school bus
drivers, food service employees, students, parents, and others recognize needs and seek assistance in different areas of the education
and the public education enterprise; and each group or individual
is either assisted adequately by some person or group with adequate means to achieve the end goal or does not receive adequate
assistance for satisfying important needs. A state or school district
employee, a school administrator or educator, for example, may be
meticulous about fulfilling state, federal, or local requirements, yet
fail substantially at meeting various needs of peers or subordinates
who are each part of relationships across the education enterprise.

7. When the challenge named is "community" . . . Particular
challenges may arise, or be anticipated, that lead to reactions or
responses focused around community. Challenges related to a
community can vary from severe to minor. Such challenges may
have components of economic, ethnic, intellectual, geographic, or
population factors that inhibit (or, conversely, that create advantages related to) educational opportunities. Additional educational
opportunities can be either advanced or inhibited in communities
due to higher or lower levels of mutuality, collegiality, and trust, in
contrast to relationships that are highly fractious and adversarial.

Although, to the extent that citizen-leadership and participants are accustomed to tough negotiations and constructive political give-and-take, friction can create positive rather than negative results in community systems and life.

8. When the challenge named is "tradition" or "innovation" . . . Particular challenges may arise, or be anticipated, that lead to reactions/responses focused around tradition and innovation. Distinguishing between trendiness and innovation is important, as is distinguishing between dynamic, positive strategic efforts building onto healthy tradition and repeating the same thing in hopes of achieving different (and more positive) results, the latter of which, in contemporary lay psychology, is one definition of insanity. At least one renowned educator tells of consulting first, with certain educators (administrators and classroom teachers) who, at least at the time, prohibited all personal electronic devices in the classroom setting and second, with others who selectively call upon students to utilize the computer, Internet, and app possibilities of these devices. The first group mostly judges personal electronic devices as distracting, trendy, and highlighting play rather than more traditional understanding and practice. The second group (with appropriate prohibitions against personal communication and off-topic use during class) judges the same devices as innovations that facilitate collaboration, teamwork, expedited research, and expanded creative spheres (particularly where a school has too few computer resources per student enrolled).[2]

9. When the challenge named is "choice" . . . Particular challenges may arise, or be anticipated, that lead to reactions or responses focused around choice. Choice has been very much in play as a dynamic since the mid-1960s, when, in certain regions, some citizens sought options beyond the federally mandated desegregation of public schools, as required by the 1954 US Supreme Court decision in *Brown v. Board of Education*. Race and desegregation, therefore, have historically been factors in arguments for being able to choose what school one's child attends. This can affect

2. Ladsen-Billings, personal interview, October 2012.

public schools with a certain talent drain as parents pull students out of public school systems and enroll them in private or independent schools.

Choosing to switch a child's enrollment to a private or independent school while continuing to live in the same public school district has no direct effect on the public school's tax-base and income unless a state legislature creates a tax exemption, tax-credit, or voucher-allowance to spare those households from having to pay public school taxes while the household's adults pay tuition for one or more children to attend a private or independent school.

Financially, public schools have been affected directly by choice when families or businesses move out of a given school district. Eventually property values can decline, tax revenues can decline, and a financial and enrollment crisis can develop.

One may rightly argue that choosing to move to a more affluent area for schooling or to relocate a business for any number of reasons is a fundamental individual constitutional right. There is no question about this.

Choice is here included, though, as a challenge reaction or response dynamic that significantly influences short-term and long-term quality education elements. This choice dynamic, therefore, requires consideration in this orientation assessment, and it merits the creation of proactive positive plans and developments to compete with other choices, as Wolfe and Skocpol have concluded and urged.[3] As one illustration, public school districts have sought—with district-wide parent-constituents—to build up and build in options for choice within their districts through the establishment of public-charter, magnet, and specialty schools that are not limited in enrollment to area-specific, designated boundaries.

10. When the challenge named is "authoritarianism" . . . Particular challenges may arise, or be anticipated, that lead to reactions or responses focused around authoritarianism. Generally speaking, authoritarianism, as an approach-perspective, is a means in

---

3. See Wolfe, *Moral Freedom*, 228–29, 230; Skocpol, *Diminished Democracy*, 240–41, 292–93.

means-to-ends considerations. As a style or mode of leadership, authoritarianism vests final (and sometimes initial) authority in a single, executive-type leader. Authoritarian leadership cultivates little or no shared leadership or collaboration up and down the line with a system's constituents.

Frequently this style develops when a high ranking administrator, a school board, or a supervising state agency decides that current leadership at a particular school or district has been ineffective in reversing precipitous declines, or has failed to implement directed or directional changes. Also, school boards have been known to choose—at least for a given term of office—a superintendent with a strong personality and authorize the individual to take the district's reins in such ways that the goals can be implemented almost immediately. At least in the first several weeks or months, the board endorses the new superintendent and such an action plan.

All of us need to acknowledge how some collateral fall-out is part of leadership change and of a system's course alteration. If someone's plan for change leaves victims in its wake, serious evaluative considerations need to be undertaken. A potential major downside casualty in such situations is morale among administration, faculty, and students. More than one person has observed what's called the three year cycle with strong-personality and authoritarian superintendents (and others in leadership roles). It has been said, "They spend one year installing their system, one year overseeing and managing what they've installed, and a third year looking for another job. Then the cycle starts all over again."[4]

Both in the situations where a school board voluntarily chooses a superintendent with a strong personality and an authoritarian style, and in the situations when a state agency for various reasons mandates and appoints for a district a superintendent, the new superintendent enters the picture with little or no positive feeling for the community, except that it is a problem to be fixed.

4. From interviews conducted with an urban middle school teacher in May 2013 and with an urban school board member in September 2013.

This is not to say that such a plan is never positive for a district or community. To the extent that calamitous, intransigent situations exist, turnarounds are important. Thinking that a substantial expanse of time exists to implement change is self-deceptive. Even so, healthy, respectful collegiality, where colleagues are willing to work together in systemic problem-solving, holds the better potential than authoritarian means. In extremely unhealthy challenges, finding a negotiated middle-ground that seeks community-wide input and buy-in is most likely a preferred course.

11. When the challenge named is "personnel" . . . Particular challenges may arise, or be anticipated, that lead to reactions or responses focused around personnel. These identifiable challenges may present themselves in a variety of ways, but most common is an approach-perspective that either (a) seeks evaluation of personnel with a primary goal being elimination of chronically underperforming employees; or (b) seeks evaluation of personnel with the improvement of all employees as a primary goal.

This is no argument that underperforming employees are not a drain on the system and on a system's morale. It is, however, an argument that employee evaluation steps which arguably have a presumptive outcome in setting a bar for likely unattainable empirical improvement are badly disguised efforts that actually intimidate and threaten employees with termination, reassignment, or undesirable transfers. Such a means-to-ends tactic holds little possibility for a satisfactory or positive long-term outcome; then, again, was that really the goal? In such situations, the system or the lead administrator seeking faculty or staff employee changes knows full well that she or he would be nothing but lucky if the subordinate or employee who is judged to be unsatisfactory were to successfully turn around the situation without any positive, cooperative effort from the supervisor. (There is the old saying: "I'd rather be lucky than good;" yet it is never the preferred way to operate a school or school system!)

In areas where strong educator unions or strong educator associations exist, school districts, boards, administrators, and classroom educators are frequently compelled by contract to follow standing protocols in employment and personnel policy matters. Whether or not strong educator associations or unions exist to give support to educators and classroom teachers in personnel matters, high turnover among both faculty and administrators is a personnel challenge that creates, of course, lack of continuity and chips away at team-building among a functioning education community. Economic considerations and available funding also affect personnel.

In many, if not most settings, employees with more experience are more highly paid than employees with less experience, thus creating, in given situations, the temptation to place experience lower on the importance scale in filling vacated positions. This, logically, can place dollars to be saved higher on the importance scale and, therefore, weight the scales in the hiring decision in favor of the candidate for the position who has fewer years' experience.

Negative critiques of legislated teacher tenure have also become part of public debates and polarized talking points through which educator unions and associations have been accused of defending poor or unmotivated teachers or administrators. An under-30 teacher in a state with an in-place educator tenure system has written:

> Even though it is the administrator's place to grant tenure, the teachers union has still found ways to get involved. Currently tenure is protecting low-performing teachers from ever being fired and is encouraging complacency among the vast majority of educators. Part of the reason I left public education for a faculty position in a charter school is because I was tired of working alongside teachers who were apathetic, not open to professional growth, and only concerned with increasing their pay. I was also tired of watching the teachers who were doing the least amount of work continue to be brainwashed by the teachers' union that they were "victims."

That's one young professional's assessment. It does not make what she identifies universally applicable or even accurate, but it is her observation.[5]

5. From an interview with an urban classroom teacher, currently serving

Teach for America (TFA, mentioned earlier, under "contexts") is an innovative and positive program allowing recent bachelor's-degree graduates, in any number of study concentrations and majors, an opportunity for immediate employment and specific educator training and accountability through partnerships between TFA and districts that contract with them. Since these districts most often are high challenge areas of service, the partnership of TFA and these districts creates an opportunity for recent university graduates, who are approved as program participants, to give back in service through working in these situations where energetic new educators are needed, and through which the districts and the students also benefit.

As with any good-faith effort, legitimate critiques exist about TFA, critiques which may be anecdotal—and are arguably dismissable for that reason—yet which also are understandable, if not logical and predictable. Three such critiques follow.

a. "While there have been some statistical gains in student testing results [where TFA is a district contract partner], some say this is not conclusive."[6]

b. Local and longer-time educators have said, "TFA new colleagues are here for two years, and then they're gone."

c. "We find some TFA new colleagues are reluctant to bond with the existing faculty." Contributing to the community aspect of both the academic and the residential community might not be very high on the list of some TFA employees' priorities, due to their term-specific commitment of two years, and since they are not from the community where they are assigned. It would not, for this reason, be unnatural for some to have an outlook like, "Do the time. Move on up the line."

---

in a charter school, who has special education training related to students with learning challenges.

6. Farr, Kopp, and Kamras, *Teaching As Leadership*, 216–17, 235.

Obviously in the examples of the previous paragraph, neither anecdotal vignettes nor broad-brush generalizations constitute hard data. Even hypothetically, however, these examples indicate how personnel challenges create reactions and responses that have implications and that are a mix of positive and negative.

12. When the challenge named is "national and international citizen formation" . . . Particular challenges may arise, or be anticipated, that lead to reactions or responses focused around national and international citizen formation. This approach-perspective considers students as citizens of communities that are local, regional, national, and global. Those who advance this general approach-perspective, however, weigh differently a variety of priorities and considerations.

    a.   If a priority and even the end goal is competitiveness and supremacy in relation to the preparedness of students of other nations, then education efforts frequently focus on national goals for student (and faculty) achievement and proficiency. STEM schools (science, technology, engineering, and mathematics) and the derivative E-STEM schools (adding economics) are substantial contributors to this effort. Many argue that the failure to be anything less than top tier in comparison to the ability and proficiency of other nations literally creates a national security crisis.[7]

    b.   Others within the United States argue with equal passion for emphases that include the more classical or liberal education curricula. These advocates promote both content and analytical proficiency in subjects such as literature, history, fine arts, languages, even individual and team sports. Their case is based on the reasoning that creativity is as crucial for problem solving as it is for individual artistic expression. Yes, STEM (and E-STEM) schools can emphasize

7. See American Academy of Arts and Sciences, "The Heart of the Matter"; and Ravitch, "Do Our Public Schools Threaten National Security?"

problem solving directly within the areas of science, technology, engineering, and mathematics (and including economics); yet certain professionals in these subject areas articulate arguments emphasizing how international competitors of the United States have been heard saying that they particularly value the creative problem solving ability of the United States' educated workers. Those foreign science and technology experts attribute the source of their positive observation to the US's historically multidisciplinary curricula.

c. A third contribution to the approach-perspective addressing a need for US students to navigate astutely and function well in roles as international citizens is curricula within schools that emphasize foreign languages and even study-abroad and exchange opportunities, where financial means exist to support this. Such curricular possibilities may additionally occur, in public systems, through magnet school or even language-specialty select school offerings and opportunities.

d. A fourth contributor promoting education that develops international citizen capability is technology itself, which can facilitate global learning opportunities and exchanges on a broad scale, where a desired foreign emphasis is streamed electronically into a learning setting with interactive potential.

As stated earlier, these twelve topics do not comprehensively identify all challenges faced by education systems, either public or private. This selective list is, however, broad enough for citizen stakeholders to develop an analytical sense related to crucial issues faced and current efforts to react and respond to such challenges.

In the following chapter, we shall explore eleven questions that face education systems (and public education, in particular) and that face the public in the endeavor of serving and striving toward the common good. The questions involve topics that are less complex in certain considerations and more complex in other considerations. Hearing these eleven questions, anyone can have multiple and even inconsistent opinions, often shaped variously by personal experience or by what others say; and sometimes opinions and perspectives will change over the years. We'll listen to a number of persons who frequently demonstrate substantially differing opinions, on the way (we hope) to being more positively engaged ourselves for the common good.

Chapter 8

Eleven Questions Related to Public Education for the Common Good

SINCE AT LEAST THE post–Civil War decades, children, teens, and adults have played, with some variations, an American parlor game called Twenty Questions. In each round or sequence, the person in the role of "It" serves as the initiator and focus-player. He or she thinks of a subject-answer for the round, not shared with the other players, that "It" writes down on a piece of paper to be revealed at the end of the round. "It" then receives questions, one at a time from the other participants, all of this in anticipation that one of the questioners will ask a question that correctly names what "It" has written on the paper.

The questions and inquiries are traditionally framed so that the answers from "It" are given in one-word replies, including "yes," "no," "both," or "neither." When a questioner correctly guesses the subject-answer for that round, "It" shows the written pre-round topic, and the correct questioner then becomes "It" for the succeeding round. Should the twentieth question of a round be asked without a correct guess, the person who has served as "It" continues in the same role for another round, or that role, through some process, is given to another participant for the succeeding round.

Methodologically, this game employs both deductive and inductive learning skills: eliminating (deductively) incorrect suppositions and utilizing (inductively) all remaining potential elements in order to establish and to narrow a developing profile toward accurately guessing the round's subject-answer.

How in the world does this pertain to public education and the common good? Consider it this way: Within public education there are so many challenges, so many opinions and perspectives, and so many combinations of those in given contexts, that it is literally impossible for a single recipe or fix to exist. Yet to expand and enhance citizen stakeholders' awareness of what might and might not be included in healthy combinations of goals, strategies, and resources, let's format this chapter as an abbreviated form of that parlor game, calling this effort, Eleven Questions. In our version, ten questions deductively and inductively will lead to the eleventh inquiry, which, sneaking a peek onto "It's" piece of paper, could be asked this way: "Is the subject-answer for today's game, 'A positive public education for the common good'?" The answer to this prematurely disclosed eleventh question, we hope, is, "Yes!"

Before we begin, let's remember how a game format, as a metaphor, can be helpful, understanding that the real-life enterprise and set of endeavors with a goal of positive public education for the common good is undeniably no game at all. It is life-givingly serious, because the lives of individuals and communities are on the line every day.

As has been written and asserted: positive public education for the common good is a complex goal for anyone to pursue and seek to accomplish. Moreover, there are no magic wands, no genies in lamps or bottles, no silver bullets from which healthy and constructive changes can be achieved or instituted, either instantaneously or over a brief period of time, such as a year or two or three. Nothing of such a nature exists.

Diane Ravitch acknowledges how all of us, herself included, can be drawn to embrace, for a time, "fads, movements, and reforms which invariably distract us from the steadiness of purpose needed to improve our schools."[1]

Imagine attempting to assemble a picture-puzzle of only ten square, interchangeable pieces portraying varied colors. Imagine also that before you could decide where the ninth and tenth pieces fit to complete the picture, you realized that the colors on the second and fourth pieces have mysteriously changed, and they should perhaps be in the positions of the third and seventh pieces. When you make that alteration, however, the fifth and sixth pieces you previously placed seem to have experienced a color-change and might blend better in the first and eighth positions. Even when the puzzle and its pieces seem to have the possibility of a completed finish, the puzzle colors mysteriously can change.

Even if we who assemble a color-changing puzzle think the puzzle ought to lend itself to completion, it never does. Similarly, with education—as with life—a static or fixed arrangement of pieces will not work next week or next year, because the pieces themselves change. This can be maddening for us, or we can become more skilled because we know the nature of the puzzle, and we learn "steadiness" (Ms. Ravitch's term) in experiencing the changes around and within us.

Returning to the analogy employed in earlier chapters, different orchestra conductors rehearsing even the same symphonic arrangement will have in common a pursuit of excellence for the concert; but they will prepare their musicians according to the respective method and style each conductor prefers. Recognizing there are multiple trails through the forest, as there are multiple ways to prepare an orchestra for an upcoming concert or series of concerts, let's consider ten questions that, we hope, will lead to a good outcome, namely, being able to identify a positive public education for the common good (please see appendix E for a question-and-answer outline of this material).

1. The person, "It," is asked: "Is ideology involved?"
     Answer for the game of Eleven Questions: "Yes."

---

1. Ravitch, *Death and Life*, 3.

The ideology (or ideologies) may be political, religious, economic, sociological, or educational in nature. By "ideology" in this first question, and in the following second question, I mean "a philosophical basis and goal which comprise an agenda intended to prevail in the midst of others, including prevailing through any need to engage and defeat whatever rivals may pose a challenge." Such ideologies shape educational components and trajectories mainly to serve the ideology itself. The endeavor of education, including public education, therefore, takes the shape of and/or reflects the look, personality, and goals of a primary ideology held by a given person. This is not necessarily negative, but, as a factor of influence, being able to recognize and analyze someone else's ideology (and one's own) is crucial for our constructive engagement with one another—as partners, one hopes, but, as can unfold, also as adversaries.

Particular means to broader ends and goals may become ideological essentials to a person's or a group's programmatic efforts, even though the broad end goal may not accurately be classified as an ideology. Examples include high stakes, results-based testing, textbook content, and school choice or private school vouchers. These may be means to ends, such as students' successful content-and-process mastery and completion of high achievement standards; yet proponents of such means may advocate for and insist on the particular component's inclusion being so high in prioritization that there is little doubt that the proponents have created an ideological win-lose issue, to the degree that the ideological component becomes a litmus test for validation of overall support of education.

Diane Ravitch comments on how means can be ideologically driven, even while ends, such as egalitarian, high-quality education, "are shaped by ideologues and egalitarians alike." She adds a personal example of a major change of perspective that she experienced in her professional judgment and direction: "I came to the realization that free markets coupled with test-based accountability would not solve our education ills, and actually risked making them worse."[2]

2. The person, "It," is asked: "If destructive stress exists where ideology is present, is the ideology (or, are the ideologies) involved a virus or a vitamin?"

Answer for the game of Eleven Questions: "A virus."

If any means or end is viewed as win-lose or as validating or invalidating, in and of itself, the potential for collateral damage is heightened. While situations in which collateral damage is a cost of doing business or a negative side-effect must be absorbed as a factor in moving forward, destructive stress and win-lose contexts and strife are generally to be judged as less than acceptable.

Even a point of view as strongly held as the public education thesis of this primer —though having evolved, one hopes, through careful study and consideration—should not become ideological in the sense that I, as the author, (or anyone else) seek to defeat, banish, or eliminate others who are advocates or proponents of choice. Escalation of ideological tensions drains resources and focus from the various quests undertaken to accomplish crucial tasks and achieve crucial goals.

Of this, E. D. Hirsch writes: "The first step in moving toward greater social justice through education is toward the premature polarizations that arise when educational policy is confused with political ideology." Hirsch explores ideology in general, and ideologies in particular, considering the direction(s) and the distance(s) toward which those who embrace and/or advance particular ideologies "succeed" and/or are influential. His own bias, for example, is for the advancement of "mainstream research, constructivism, thinking skills, 'real-world' competency, higher order thinking, and consensus research on pedagogy."[3]

In Gail Collins' book, *As Texas Goes: How the Lone Star State Highjacked the American Agenda*, she details various incidents (I'm sorry to report; but she is correct, I think) of governmental and

2. Ibid., 243.
3. Hirsch, *The Schools We Need and Why*, 5, 69–126, 127–75.

cultural lunacy, among them the intrusion of ideological agendas into State Board of Education textbook approval debates.[4]

Additionally (and bridging to upcoming questions #3 and #4 of the ten under consideration), Peter Brimelow and Steve Perry, among others, have argued ideologically (and, they would say, personally and from their own experience) about obstructionism practiced by classroom educators' collective associations (or unions). They assert that such collective associations so extensively and self-interestedly serve the interests of educators in matters such as compensation, tenure, and resistance to reform, that educators' collective associations fail to serve the educational enterprise faithfully.[5]

In the system that is ours (as some say, "The world as it is, not as we wish it were"), neither passivity nor conquest and vanquishing efforts get us where we need to be. There are, however, ways and methods by which competing ideologies can co-exist—not peacefully, necessarily, but respectfully, at least. A positive public education for the common good depends on such respect coexisting, albeit in respectfully adversarial political environments, in which, via debate, civil arguments, and votes, citizen stakeholders seek the always-moving target that is the common good.

An exemplary qualification to the general answer "It" gave to the second of the eleven questions—that ideological stirring and fostering of negative stress is a virus—may be found in Neil Postman's broad sense of a narrative (perhaps, meta-narrative) that affirms pluralism in United States schools and educational endeavors[6], and which can function as a "vitamin" ideology.

3. The person, "It," is asked: "Are teachers and their collective voices involved?"

Answer for the game of Eleven Questions: "Yes."

Many people who profess an interest in education reform have heard someone, somewhere say that teachers and classroom

4. Collins, *As Texas Goes*, 112–15.

5. Brimelow, *The Worm in the Apple*, 3; Perry, *Push Has Come to Shove*, 137–69.

educators are everything from part of the problem to obstruction- ists in the quest to reform public education. It should suffice to say that no multilayered organization can thrive or be sustained with- out at least twelve characteristics: mutual respect, collaboration, teamwork, cooperation, compromise, candor, honesty, empathy, sympathy, commitment, sacrifice, and good humor.

Day after day, innumerable educators, administrators, and support staff share these dozen positive qualities (and more!) in countless contexts across semesters and years. Every semester and every year problems and challenges arise. Adversarial relation- ships, contentious dealings, and bitter rivalries aid no one.

This is not to say that educational settings—including pub- lic education settings—can exist positively without conflict. As most sociologists and group dynamics experts have observed and taught, when conflict develops, something of value is at stake. Often conflict develops among classroom educators themselves, between classroom educators and administrators, and with public employees and elected officials, from school board members to politicians to education department personnel at all levels: local, state, and federal.

One method of dealing with conflict has been for administra- tors and public officials to diminish, ignore, or oppose classroom teacher associations or unions. The direct and indirect results of such efforts create and exacerbate rivalries and hostility. In contrast, when administrators and public officials view classroom teachers as partners on a common team, strides forward can be experienced, challenges met, and quality results and relationships observed. No system with human beings involved is ever perfect; yet no system needs to be perpetuated with a norm of relationships that are more uncooperative and disrespectful than they are positive and func- tioning daily to foster professional and personal respect for all par- ticipants, including students and parents. All of us as adults do well to ask ourselves: How can students be expected to grow in respect and team-building skills and roles with fellow students and adults if non-constructive and unmediated contentiousness is the norm among their mentors at the place where they learn?

4. The person, "It," is asked: "Are teachers and classroom educators—individually and collectively—best understood as solution inhibitors or solution contributors?"

Answer for the game of Eleven Questions: "Solution contributors."

Administrators whose first instinct in relation to classroom educators is adversarial and irritated either initiate, re-kindle, or perpetuate anger and resistance within the system of a school or a district. The same applies to teachers in their attitudes toward administrators. Administrators have told of experiences with classroom teachers and their collective associations who, they say, spend more time protecting ineffective and tenured colleagues than they spend seeking positive solutions to negative and threatening influences that challenge the best efforts of others at the school.

While Michelle Rhee is critical of educators' collective associations and unions,[6] her criticism seems less severe than Perry's and Brimelow's (mentioned previously). Countering those views, however, Diane Ravitch, Mark Simon, and Randi Weingarten assert that "due process" and respect for educator colleagues are essential for systemic health, confidence, morale, and progress in building the education community team. Administrators, school board members, politicians, and others who ignore this positive consideration do all citizen stakeholders a disservice.

Equally so, from the other side, when a collegial educators' association or union obstructs efforts for enhancement of education services that could benefit students and families simply due to the fact that the educator's association or union does not have control of the steering wheel of the vehicle bringing change, then, yes, in that situation, the collective association would be a solution inhibitor.

Rhee states the issue this way:

> "In order to ensure that every kid has a highly effective teacher, we have to differentiate among teachers. We

6. Rhee, *Radical*, 201–64.

have to have a rigorous evaluation system that deter-
mines which teachers have the greatest success with kids
and which do not. It also necessitates that we intervene
with those who are not performing. We either quickly
improve their skills and capabilities or we move them
out of the system, because our kids cannot afford to be
taught by an ineffective teacher . . . (This) elevates the
teaching profession; (and) it ensures that we're putting
students and their interests first – above job security and
tenure for teachers. That's not anti-teacher; it's pro-kid."[7]

All too often, however, in a desire to shortcut or short-circuit
a process for improvement that is not immediate, instantaneous, or
short-term, administrators and public officials have been known
to choose quicker-fix methods to shake up personnel, offset defi-
cits, balance budgets, and streamline the route toward their goals.
Given those perceived needs and means, reducing paid personnel
along with reducing student, family, and faculty support services
are a few of the options of easiest resort.

Ravitch notes how the Bill and Melinda Gates Foundation has
contributed financially to both educators' collective associations
and to high stakes and charter school efforts, eventually preferring
the high stakes and charter efforts to the exclusion of educators'
collective associations.[8] She also notes that some of the first charter school efforts were begun by classroom educators (and union
members) who were seeking alternate ways and methods by which
student progress might be enhanced. Many such efforts, however,
were abandoned when charter efforts began succumbing to the
overshadowing influence of entrepreneurs, foundations, administrators, and public officials who desired a system and environment
free of collective educators' associations and unions, for reasons of
both reduced compensation and the disenfranchisement of employee influences.[9]

---

7. Ibid., 214–15.

8. Ravitch, *Death and Life*, 276–77.

9. Ibid., 122–25.

Mark Simon, in an essay entitled "High-Stakes Progressive Teacher Unionism," defies the stereotype that many anti-union educators, administrators, and citizen stakeholders describe. An National Education Association (NEA) leader who began as a classroom educator, Simon outlines his convictions for education reform that benefits students and that holds both classroom educators (association and union members) and administrators accountable for the best professionalism possible, which means keeping all students' learning possibilities as the utmost priority.

He writes: "It is the duty of each teacher union elected leader and each staff person to have a plan that envisions a better school system, better schools, and correctives to misdirected accountability strategies—and then to fight like the dickens for that teacher vision . . . a vision that is tough on teachers. Craft unions in the nineteenth and twentieth centuries . . . were the guardians of quality control in the face of employers' tendency to try to cut corners. In education, where the decision making is complex and we're not producing widgets, craft unionism is the better model of organization."[10]

Simon and others advocate for students, faculty, parents, and administrators to be key team members of a complex educational system. Unless each group is student-focused, the likelihood of quality outcomes is severely threatened. Even with some bad apples in every barrel—the teacher barrel, the administrator barrel, the student barrel, and the parent barrel—why in the world would administrators, public officials, parents, or anyone choose to antagonize and denigrate quality development and partnership possibilities with faculty members and support staff? Can you imagine a parent making no effort to provide nutrition and maximal learning environments for his or her children? Surely it happens, but can a conscientious person imagine it? It's not that different if administrators, public officials, parents, members of the general public, or teachers and educators themselves view the educational endeavor cynically and as beyond partnership and

10. Simon, "High-Stakes Progressive Unionism" in Elmore, *I Used to Think . . . and Now I Think . . .*, 152.

collaborative, respectful, community improvement. Hostility, mistrust, and avoidance deprive our education community system of nourishment. Turnarounds only occur when we share vision and its implementation for students and their future.

Two anecdotal asides: (a) On the subject of learning environments and communitywide shared responsibility, a sign posted by the collective educators' association in a century-old elementary school building of a mid-Atlantic urban neighborhood stated: "Our teaching conditions are your child's learning conditions." (b) A very bright public charter school headmaster was speaking about the school where he served and was relieved to tell his audience that his school was the beneficiary of relief from teacher union personnel requirements and membership. He continued to say that he and his faculty strived to provide: a supportive environment; a positive attitude; clear expectations; and teachers who are encouraging of students and parents. He was stunned to be asked by one of his listeners, though, if he had read Randi Weingarten's essay in the book on education, *Waiting for Superman*, wherein Weingarten (then president of the American Federation of Teachers) writes of her professional understanding of what the best schools provide through their faculty, administration, and board: good teachers supported by good leaders; good curricula; an environment that eliminates barriers to students' success; shared responsibility and mutual accountability; and collaboration, not competition or combativeness.[11]

This is an example of two education professionals—one in an urban public-charter school, the other working from a national union office—who sound amazingly similar in what they each understand to be means for success in the endeavor of public education and the common good. Might such shared perspectives and vision be the beginning of something encouraging? Might it be contagious, in a good way? Thus, we can hope for perspectives similar to what Prime Minister Winston Churchill encouraged his fellow English citizens to adopt, saying, after the first Allied victory

11. Weingarten, "Five Foundations for Student Success," in Weber, *Waiting for Superman*, 149–60.

of World War II in North Africa: "This is not the end. It is not even the beginning of the end. It is, perhaps, though, the end of the beginning."

5. The person, "It," is asked: "Are high-stakes testing, teacher-effectiveness evaluations, and results-driven philosophies involved?"
    Answer for the game of Eleven Questions: "They can be."

As has been intimated in previous pages, this question and the one following have the capacity to create an almost Grand Canyon–sized chasm between those who hold opinions on such topics.

Steve Perry, in *Push Has Come to Shove: Getting Our Kids the Education They Deserve—Even If It Means Picking a Fight*, seems to give a confident "yes" in answer to this question. He may even be saying, "Yes, and more!" when he writes:

> "I agree . . . that test scores alone do not a good teacher make. I also agree with the Washington [DC] Teachers' Union's assertion that too few principals are aware of what a good teacher is, therefore, too few can be trusted to determine if the teacher is effective. Where [I disagree with the DC Teachers' Union] is . . . I believe that we should use standardized measures, including but not limited to students' performance tests, student evaluations of teachers, and attendance and graduation rates, as well as other observable yet not currently standardized characteristics, such as hours teachers spend leading extracurricular activities and their ability to build meaningful relationships."[12]

On this subject, Perry credits Michelle Rhee and Joel Klein with developing "comprehensive and elaborate plans" that can facilitate the identification of effective teachers.

Since such comprehensive and elaborate plans are most often adopted by a governing body at some level; this seems an appropriate place to hear Phillip Schlechty's argument from *Leading for Learning: How to Transform Schools into Learning Organizations*:

---

12. Perry, *Push Has Come to Shove*, 169.

"The fact is that state-mandated standards, especially as they are being enforced through standardized testing, are becoming the primary vehicles through which public schools are being transformed into government agencies. This results in the standards-based movement becoming a fundamental threat to the link between the public and the schools. It drives a wedge between the parents and teachers, and in the long run it will remove from local environments one of the most powerful sources for a sense of belonging and a sense of community among local residents. It is therefore not only the education of children that is at stake. The long-term health of American democracy is at stake as well, as is the vitality of the local communities on which democracy depends."[13]

From a somewhat different angle on this topic, Diane Ravitch has written: "The goal of accountability should be to support and improve schools, not the heedless destruction of careers, reputations, lives, communities, and institutions. The decision to close a school is a death sentence for an institution; it should be recognized as a worst-case scenario. The abject failure of a school represents the failure of those in charge of the district, not just the people who work in the school."[14]

Schlechty and Ravitch lead us from the "They can be" less-than-absolute answer to question #5 to consider whether high-stakes testing, teacher effectiveness evaluations, and results-driven philosophies contribute in every situation to a positive public education for the common good. They, and others, also help us move to the clearly related and more direct question, which we consider next.

6. The person, "It," is asked: "Are high-stakes testing, teacher effectiveness evaluations, and results-driven philosophies involved as the primary means for overcoming students' low achievement and enhancing the nation's future?"

Answer for the game of Eleven Questions: "No."

13. Schlechty, *Leading for Learning*, 161.
14. Ravitch, *Death and Life*, 166.

Diane Ravitch has written, "I changed my mind about means, not ends. My basic educational philosophy remained the same. I have always wished that every child might have the same high-quality education that I wanted for my children and now want for my grandchildren ... Eventually, I came to the realization that free markets coupled with test-based accountability would not solve our education ills, and actually risked making them worse."[15]

She recalls the histories of the US Department of Education program themes during the George W. Bush and Barack Obama administrations, first, "No Child Left Behind," then, "Race to the Top," and how both efforts, representing the rising tide of education reform, created adversarial side effects and negative consequences. Ravitch notes: "Unlike dissident school reform movements of the past, this one had the support of the nation's wealthiest foundations, corporate executives, Wall Street hedge fund managers, leaders of the technology sector, and the top elected officials of both major political parties ... The movement asserted that [United States] education was failing and that this failure was due to the large numbers of 'bad teachers' ... " Ravitch adds to her assessment comments relating how strategic and tactical mechanisms of change—as determined by the "new reform advocates"—advocated school choice, charter schools, non-unionized educators, and standardized test scores for measuring success and failure on the part of students, their teachers, their administrators, and their schools.[16]

In early 2012, the Council on Foreign Relations (CFR) published a paper by Joel I. Klein, Condoleezza Rice, and others, entitled "US Education Reform and National Security."[17]

In *The New York Review of Books*, Ravitch critiques the CFR paper, noting, "What marks this report as different from its predecessors (which have also been critical of the state of education in the United States) ... is its profound indifference to the role of public

15. Ibid., 243.
16. Ibid., 250.
17. Klein and Rice, "U.S. Education Reform and National Security."

education in a democratic society and its certainty that private organizations will succeed where the public schools have failed."[18]

Sixteen years earlier, E. D. Hirsch Jr., argued that certain basic principles of learning "apply universally," including "the distinction between primary and secondary learnings; the importance of early beginnings; the need for effort and practice; and the need to automate operations and develop relevant intellectual capital to overcome the limitations of short-term memory and the cumulative nature of learning."[19]

He then added: "Moreover, when [these] are put into practice in teaching large numbers of children in large systems of education, the possible ways of applying them effectively and fairly begin to narrow."[20] Even from 1996, Hirsch is acknowledging and encouraging recognition of a reality that is articulated far too infrequently: The greater the numbers or the greater the complexity, the greater the challenges and their attendant difficulties.

As answered in question #5 of this Eleven Questions game, high-stakes testing, teacher-effectiveness evaluations, and results-driven philosophies can be—and actually are—involved in the enterprise and endeavor under discussion. The Eleven Questions game answer to question # 6, however—"Are high-stakes testing, teacher-effectiveness evaluations, and results-driven philosophies involved as the primary means for overcoming students' low achievement and enhancing the nation's future?"—is "No." These are means but are best not considered primary means. This distinction is asserted because nothing can equal or surpass the primacy of the students themselves and their communities of care and citizenship. Their engaged citizenship and their journey toward the goal of that engaged citizenship are ends, yes; but when these ends are continually being personalized, they are also the means.

In 2009, Phillip Schlechty wrote in his book, *How to Transform Schools into Learning Organizations*, ". . . educational leaders who are committed to public education as community-building,

---

18. Ravitch, "Do Our Public Schools Threaten National Security?"

19. Hirsch, *The Schools We Need*, 236.

20. Ibid.

as well as a child-focused endeavor—and who believe that their job is building a public for public education—need a deep understanding . . . [of the mind-set against which they must contend, specifically] how and why a bureaucratic mind-set has come to dominate the thinking of America's business leaders and education policy elite—and the impact this is having on local citizens."[21]

Then, in 2011, he wrote in his successor volume, *Engaging Students: The Next Level of Working on the Work*:

> "Nowadays, the expectation is that the young will learn to pursue intellectual matters with discipline and delight, [and] that the schools will provide for nearly every child a form of education that [the culture] once assumed only the elite could [receive]. Superintendents, principals, and teachers must hold themselves accountable for providing such an elite education for nearly every child. They must face the fact that the government-sponsored systems of accountability, in which they are now trapped, confuse mediocrity with excellence and test scores with standards. Schools and those who work in them must approach their task very differently from the past. They must set direction rather than follow directions; they must invent the future rather than simply cope with a future that is thrust on them."[22]

7. The person, "It," is asked: "Are school choice and select schools necessarily involved in this endeavor?"

Answer for the game of Eleven Questions: "No. Not necessarily. Certainly not exclusively."

As we have already discussed, freedom to choose where one's child will attend school, either within a public school district or across district boundaries, is where we are in the United States. This is not necessarily bad or negative for public education advocates. Other independent education options are not only constitutional, these other options can serve as incentives for public education staying up as much as successful public education can serve as an

21. Schlechty, *Leading for Learning*, 158.
22. Schlechty, *Engaging Students*, 185–86.

incentive to independent educational options and choosers—in theory, at least.[23]

Choice options within districts can be mostly positive at secondary levels where specialty academic tracks are offered, such as with magnet schools. Choice options within districts at elementary levels, however, let districts off the hook when public officials and administrators endorse or insist on strategic and tactical plans resulting in talent drains on particular neighborhood schools. The argument, for example, from "No Child Left Behind" and "Race to the Top" advocates has often been phrased: "Parents and their children should not be forced to support and attend 'failing schools.'" Again, in theory, this is absolutely understandable.

Both vouchers for independent education options (which assist with tuition discounts funded through public education financial resources) and public resource financing of charter schools, however, drain the total treasury assets that would otherwise be available for distribution among the general public system and districts.

Sanctioned choice options are both legal and important unless and until the public effort for public education obligations and general commitments are diminished. Beginning at that point, however, choice and select schools set in motion factors and influences that detract from a robust public system with a fighting chance to overcome serious challenges.

Diane Ravitch sheds light on such temptations and potentially unhelpful results through, first, tracing back the source of the voucher rationale to Milton Friedman's 1955 essay, "The Role of Government in Education," in which he argued that government's role was to "fund schooling but not run the schools."[24] Second, she explains charter schools' original purpose "for discovering better ways of educating hard-to-educate children . . . not to siphon away the most motivated students and families in the poorest communities."[25]

---

23. Hirsch, *The Schools We Need*, 60–63.
24. Ravitch, *Death and Life*, 114.
25. Ibid., 146.

8. The person, "It," is asked: "Is more public funding involved?"
Answer for the game of Eleven Questions: "Likely always."

Someone has said, "If money can fix your problem, then you don't really have a problem." While I understand that in terms of a hail-damaged automobile or a computer hard-drive crash (provided, in the second case, that everything was backed up on an external hard drive), there are at least two deficiencies in such reasoning. One deficiency is that there certainly can be severe shortages of money. So anyone may have a substantial problem develop and possess no fiscal resources for the replacement needed. The second deficiency is the one predicted: even unlimited money cannot fix some problems and challenges. A chronic illness, a permanently physically or mentally impairing injury, or a fatal incident cannot be fixed with money, no matter how great one's financial reserves.

If money could guarantee a fix to all challenges that every classification of education faces or which public education specifically faces, it might be possible to solicit and gather the funding to address and overcome the challenges. But even if adequate funding could overcome the immeasurable challenges, which it cannot, different challenges would crop up. Due to the evolving nature of life, new challenges flare up with more predictability than hot spots following a major fire.

What's more, in our public education systems, funds are most often primarily local, secondarily state, and thirdly federal. Since tax bases in respective jurisdictions vary within states and across the nation, the average expenditure of available funds per student ranges substantially. Efforts in the direction of equalization of funding per student are both political and judicial in nature. Local school boards call elections for public authorization of tax rate levels or bond sales. State legislative bodies enact laws related to state administration boards (such as state boards of education) that may or may not be authorized by state law to render rulings related to tax assessments, collections, and distribution. Moreover, the scope and content of some of these roles and responsibilities, especially the responsibility to decide upon and exercise a role in per-student funding equalization, may be authorized for such boards and agencies in certain states to determine, or may not be. The judicial role in school funding is most noticeable in equalization disputes. Rulings and verdicts by state and federal courts vary due to the particulars of cases filed and the constitutional, statutory, and case law that applies across the jurisdiction in question. For example, one might think that the US Constitution, under the equal protection clause of the Fourteenth Amendment, suggests that students have a constitutional right to public education opportunities that would be, should be, or are to be funded under some sort of equalization formula. This is not necessarily so.

In 1973, the US Supreme Court ruled, in a 5 to 4 decision, that a three-judge federal district court had erred in deciding that the Texas state funding policy was unconstitutional. In *Savage Inequalities: Children in America's Schools*, Jonathan Kozol offers a compelling assessment of this case, which was originally consolidated with the title, *Rodriguez v. State of Texas*, and, on appeal, became *San Antonio Independent School District v. Rodriguez*. Clearly, Kozol's evaluative comments are favorable to the dissenting opinion written by Justice Thurgood Marshall, and his comments are unfavorable toward the majority opinion, which was written by Justice Lewis Powell.[26]

In Kozol's opinion, Justice Marshall captured the essence of the issue of gross disparity in funding mechanisms and formulas when poorer districts are compared to more affluent districts; and Justice Powell (Kozol believes) failed to grasp the subtleties that, taken together, create an overwhelming argument favorable to the *Rodriguez* plaintiffs. Kozol first quotes Justice Powell: "We [the Court] have no indication that [the Texas funding] system fails to provide each child with an opportunity to acquire the basic skills necessary [for] full participation in the political process [of community, state, and nation]".[27]

In his written opinion for the majority, Justice Powell was responding to a prominent angle argued by the *Rodriguez* attorney

26. Kozol, *Savage Inequalities*, 206–9.
27. Ibid., 215.

that took the legal position that gross inequities in funding actually violate students' lifelong opportunities to full participation as citizens, a right guaranteed by the Fourteenth Amendment to the US Constitution. Justice Powell additionally wrote: "Experts are divided [concerning] the extent to which there is a demonstrable correlation between educational expenditures and the quality of education."[28]

Justice Marshall, mincing no words in his dissent, which was favorable to the *Rodriguez* case's attorneys, described as "a sham" the State of Texas attorneys' argument supporting local district control of financing. Why? Because (Justice Marshall observed and opined) local districts and their citizen-voters cannot choose the level of quality education due to wide disparities in the factor of financial resources, "a factor over which local voters [have] no control."[29]

Kozol, as clearly as anyone can with broad generalizations, explains basic school funding among the fifty states, wherein, respectively, targeted goals of minimum basic funding are determined. States then ensure these goals will be met through supplemental funding back to districts whose own tax base fails to meet the applicable minimum or basic level. He further points out that, politically, in order to appease richer districts (and voters residing in richer districts), states may implement plans that offer other kinds of aid, either to all districts, or to districts above the minimum or basic funding levels. Hypothetically, such plans have the potential of offsetting the attempts at equalization, and may even widen the gap.[30]

Kozol deduces from such debates and instituted political, legislative, and judicial solutions that "the age-old conflict between liberty and equity is largely non-existent in (such a) setting. The wealthy districts have the first and seldom think about the second, while the very poor have neither."[31]

A 2012 case before the Arkansas State Supreme Court (*Fountain Lake School District* [also McCleskey] *v. Arkansas Department*

28. Ibid., 215, 217.
29. Ibid., 219.
30. Ibid., 208–9.
31. Ibid., 213.

of Education [ADE]), decided, in a 4–3 vote, in this way: That the ADE could not revise or change its interpretation of key education funding statutes that ADE had been interpreting correctly for several years. The results of the court decision have less to do with the state adequately funding K–12 education and more with preventing the state from confiscating local ad valorem taxes that are intended to support (with generosity) students within the district from which the ad valorem taxes are collected (at least, in Arkansas).

In this case, the plaintiffs of the Fountain Lake and Eureka Springs districts were collecting more in the first 25 mills of school taxes (URT—Uniform Rate of Taxes) than the state guaranteed as "foundation funding" for all students in the State. The ADE argued that local ad valorem taxes collected per student were "excess" and belonged to the state. The State Supreme Court rejected ADE's arguments. Interestingly, the ADE, in failing to settle this dispute outside of and prior to a final verdict by the State Supreme Court, was ruled to be: (a) over-reaching into the plaintiffs' districts' ad valorem tax revenue-pool; and (b) ignoring the other tax-related funding formulas, sources, and actual revenue that comprised the "foundational equalization funding" for students in less affluent districts.[32]

Every state (and district) varies in the potential of amounts that can be collected (rates) and in the ways funds are actually assessed, collected, and disbursed or expended. So the process is both political and economic, as related to communities, districts, and states. At times the process becomes judicial. Even then, after courts decide legal issues, they remand to political entities the responsibility for the particular implementation of their decisions under the law (or, under the law as prescribed for adjustment or change).

With scathing criticism, John Gatto laments the amounts of money expended by and for "government schools," writing, "the therapeutic community of psychologized public schooling is extremely expensive to maintain."[33] While Justice Powell asserts, with some others, that there may or may not be a demonstrable correlation between dollars spent per student and the quality of

32. McCleskey, *"School of Thought: Funding Decision Victory for Equality."*
33. Gatto, *Underground History*, 183, 358.

83

education,[34] public funding is a crucial factor in education—and public education.

Is there more than one way to assess this? Surely. Yet any assessment that minimizes factors maintaining inequities is arguably in need of evaluation and attention. Involvement—as with the *Rodriguez* plaintiffs, the *McCleskey* plaintiffs, and others—in the local and state political processes, therefore, is crucial. Money does not and cannot solve every problem; but shortages of money available for per student expenditures expand disparities. When some are encumbered by resource disparities, the whole of society loses, the whole public falls farther behind in any quest for the common good, and the locomotive of time keeps chugging down the track.

9. The person, "It," is asked: "Are challenging factors of diversity—for example, economic, ethnic, and racial variations; multiple cultural contexts and traditions; special needs, etc.—negative or positive?"

Answer for the game of Eleven Questions: "Positive."

Poverty, prejudice, and assorted inequities are deplorable. If, however, we live in the world as it is and not the world as we wish it might be, assorted challenging elements and factors exist all around us with steep inclines and exhausting responsibilities. How easy it continually is to complain and wish some version of utopia were closer at hand, or to attempt to create distance between where contexts of resource shortages and obvious adversity exist, and where contexts of camouflaged problems exist. There's nowhere that difficulties have been completely eliminated for individuals or communities.

Rather, in all places, communities, and relationships, there's the possibility that diversity, economic, ethnic, and racial variations, multiple cultural contexts and traditions, and special needs cry out for attention and respect, like dozens of coyotes scattered across a midnight landscape illumined by a full moon.

I view such challenges as positive to the degree that numerous persons (it is to be hoped) accept roles of mutuality among

34. Kozol, *Savage Inequalities*, 217.

such potentially adversarial burdens and rivals—and even among enemies—on the road toward healing and renewal.

The professional and personal debates related to diversity, economic, ethnic, and racial variations, multiple cultural contexts and traditions, and special needs frequently seek a presumed or fantasized common high ground, which can be labeled as mono-cultural or values-synthesized achievement. The mantra might be: "Succeed by someone's standards," and this can mean that "someone" represents the dominant culture, economically, ethni-cally, politically, and religiously speaking. Such an understanding encourages and endorses program titles, perhaps less like, "No Child Left Behind," and more like, "Race to the Top"—especially if one asks, "Who is defining 'the Top?'" and "What if someone falls exhausted or quits discouraged during the 'Race to the Top'?"

The previous paragraph is not intended to preface an endorsement of standard-less, totally subjectivized, or cultur-ally particularized curricula, academic content mastery, or performance-proficiency goals, all of which, in various ways, are standardized by the respective group responsible for determining the norms. Any of us, however, can affirm how measurable results help mark progress toward goals; and a person can function with the crucial awareness that several issues, challenges, and debates exist within the multiple contexts and broad categories of learning, teaching, testing, and measuring.

While extreme subjectivity in education can create an edu-cational equivalent of political anarchy, more than one style and school of thought can contribute to an individual's, a class's, a school's, a community's, and a system's improvement toward suc-cess; and success, itself, may have varying definitions and evolving, established, or accepted standards.

For example, Michelle Rhee and John Gatto offer examples of extreme contrast, while similarly arguing for the student. The distance between the two, however, could not be greater.

Rhee argues that educators "doing our jobs well" make a huge difference positively in the lives of students who face seri-ous adversity. Of this she is absolutely convinced, while equally acknowledging: "I don't believe that educators and schools can fix all of society's ills." She even flips the emphasis, writing: "While some contend that you can't have great schools in every community until you solve the problem of poverty, I would argue the opposite. In the words of my mentor, Joel Klein, 'You cannot solve the problem of poverty until you fix the public education system.'"[35]

In some ways, this perspective on a subject—such as educators' performance and effectiveness with little or no regard for extreme contingent factors such as poverty—may rightly be characterized by some as distracting and narrow, reducing a multidimensional, complex, evolving, ongoing dilemma to a chicken-or-egg sort of debate. In systems psychology terms, deciding consciously or acting unconsciously toward one member as the primary source of trouble that arises and leaving other members mostly without blame is termed as creating an "identifiable patient." In another descriptive metaphor, it's a circular argument, like a dog chasing its own tail. The chase will likely be unending; and the one who is suggesting the "correct" perspective simply says, "When you want to fix this thing, ask me. Otherwise it's going to go on and on." Phrased another way, the opinion offered seems to say, "Society should not debate and take attendant action on poverty until society takes up action on education (the identifiable patient) in the way I have determined will be best."

To Rhee's credit, however, she spins away from the less helpful aspect of quoting Mr. Klein, to summarize: "If you look at any country through any period of time, you will see that the single most effective strategy for combating generational poverty is education."[36]

John Gatto, a hundred and eighty degrees from Rhee, develops a multidimensional argument that is ideologically conservative (as is Rhee's), but which is, with a philosophically Libertarian perspective, far more systemically complex in content and nature. Gatto is convinced that students matter above all. He is equally convinced that public schools (which he often labels, "government schools") have evolved systemically into institutions that, by the

35. Rhee, *Radical*, 209–10.
36. Ibid.

very nature of being institutions, cannot ever serve a student's best developmental interests. From his experience as a once-upon-a-time award-winning educator in public schools, he argues that corporate, business, governmental, and even religious interests, from the earliest days of United States compulsory schooling, have treated students as products or means to ends that sustain multi-layered economic and political interests and institutions.[37]

A legitimate critique can be raised with respect to Gatto's individualistic approach to education and society, arguing that he seeks a world that simply will not or cannot ever again exist, so far out of the barn is our current context from the New England and colonial individuals who dreamed and worked for independence from the British Crown during the 1700s and early 1800s.

Interestingly, Gatto suggests that if we could, at a minimum, return to the 1859 perspective of Abraham Lincoln, we might find our way back to a better place for resetting the system. Gatto relies on Lincoln's reference to a "mudsill theory" of economics, wherein persons are used (enslaved or encumbered) by economic interests that seek the self-interest of the economically invested persons and institutions (the owners, who enforce others as the "mudsillers"), whereas Lincoln hoped all could soon be small proprietors, thus ending "mudsill-ism."[38] (One might ask, legitimately: Didn't Lincoln, in his effort to achieve and further liberation for individuals and the society across the entire set of the not-so-United States, rely upon a federalism that Gatto cannot tolerate in education—even if, in the process, Lincoln was attempting to reverse "mudsillism"?)

Gatto further writes: "The souls of free and independent men and women are mutilated by the necessary soullessness of corporate organization and decision-making . . . Strength, joy, wisdom are only available to those who produce their own lives; never to those who merely consume the production of others. Nothing good can come from inviting global corporations to design our

37. Gatto, *Dumbing Us Down*, 66–7.
38. Gatto, *Underground*, 366–67.

schools, any more than leaving a hungry dog to guard ham sand-wiches is a good way to protect lunches."[39]

As colorful as Gatto's language is, as sweeping as his historical analysis is, and as passionate as is his argument, there exists at least one point 360 years earlier than Lincoln's mudsill speech where one might contend that Gatto also under-evaluates a different historical character and that character's thinking. He writes: "Reformation Christianity . . . extended to all believers a conception of individual duty, individual responsibility, and a free will right to decide for oneself beyond any claims of states. John Calvin proclaimed in his *Institutes [of the Christian Religion]* that, through natural law, the judgment of conscience alone was able to distinguish between justice and injustice . . ."[40]

Undoubtedly Calvin is a linchpin thinker and actor in advancing the rationale of individual responsibility and accountability, which (in his opinion) should never be relegated to an institution such as State or Church. At the same time, however, it's critical to note that Calvin never advocated a noninstitutional church. The community of faith, as Calvin taught and advocated, includes a corporate structure of both officers and members that was never libertarian in theology or in practice. "Free thinking" (as a virtue) by individual believers was no more encouraged among Calvin's community of faith in Geneva, Switzerland, than was it encouraged from the Pope's ecclesiastical headquarters in Rome.

So, what and who is between Michelle Rhee and John Gatto in our quest to argue for the priority rank of students who are the clientele to be educated both amid and from a broad, varied, and complex societal set of communities? Three educators from the past twenty years come to mind who offer varying perspectives: Hirsch, Postman, and Ladson-Billings.

In 1996, E. D. Hirsch Jr., made his case for curricula in schools (specifically, he wrote of elementary schools) that have "a coherent, cumulative core curriculum which instills consensus values such as civic duty, honesty, diligence, perseverance, respect,

39. Ibid., 367.
40. Ibid., 180.

kindness, and independent-mindedness; which gives students a step-by-step mastery of procedural knowledge in language arts and content knowledge in civics, science, the arts, and the humanities; and which holds students, teachers, schools, and parents accountable for acceptable progress in achieving these specific year-by-year goals."[41]

John Gatto obviously has disagreed with Hirsch, given Gatto's resistance to evaluative standards that mostly measure success by conforming to what one might describe as pre-cast molds, according to bureaucratically or legislatively determined standards.

In a book published a year before Hirsch's *The Schools We Need*, Neil Postman, in *The End of Education: Redefining the Value of School*, critiques Hirsch's 1987 publication (*Cultural Literacy*) in which Hirsch made the case for all students having a higher probability of academic and economic success through the years of their lives in the United States to the extent that they would be proficient with a spectrum of content and methods that Hirsch called "cultural literacy." Eight years later, in writing *The Schools We Need*, Hirsch noted that he learned from others, who, in fact, shaped his views that cultural literacy carried too great a potential for being misunderstood; therefore, in *The Schools We Need*, he states his evolved preference for the phrase, "core knowledge."[42]

Postman specifically refers to Hirsch's efforts to name many content components of "cultural/core knowledge," which are said to be reflective of diversity in US culture. Postman's deviation from Hirsch, though, lies in his preference for organizing learning and curricula around multiple narratives to be evaluated and adapted, rather than facts to be digested.[43]

Specifically related to cultural, racial, and ethnic diversity, Postman mentions his personal agreement with Dr. Cornel West, and then adds: "[We must] provide ourselves and especially our young with a comprehensive narrative that makes a constructive

---

41. Hirsch, *The Schools We Need*, 236.
42. Ibid., 13.
43. Postman, *The End of Education*, 74–5.

and unifying use of diversity."[44] What does this mean, exactly? Perhaps it is not enough to be able to quote statistics on slavery or to cite incidents from the life of Harriet Tubman or Martin Luther King Jr., if this is the extent of a student's capability as a product or end-result of the education experience. More importantly, and crucial to Postman, is the developed ability for students (and adults!) to learn both component facts and developmental contexts and interpolations related to race, ethnicity, and diversity in the United States, in such ways that the multiple narratives coming forward can be appreciated for the humanity and struggle they represent and convey.

Postman includes a chapter that he entitles "The Law of Diversity," explaining: "I am keeping in mind that the purpose of public education is to help the young transcend individual identity by finding inspiration in a story of humanity."[45] This, understandably, to the extent it can be accomplished, can be considered a positive contribution toward the common good.

Before concluding this section on diversity within classrooms, school districts, and the nation and the role diversity plays every day in the world as it is, let us note a published critique of Hirsch's common core, published on August 18, 2013. *New York Times* op-ed columnist, Bill Keller, in "War on the Core," endorsed federal, state, and local efforts to advance a core knowledge, common ground, programmatic approach and framework for regional and local jurisdictions to adopt. Related to his title focused on opposition to the core, Keller noted his estimation that minimal to moderate resistance exists from the political and ideological left, but he skips past this to concentrate his pointed critique at "right-wingers" who oppose "national standards" and any advance of what they judge to be "federalism." As if he were referring specifically to John Gatto's critiques, Keller is likely accurate with this particular assessment, since he thinks this opposition is concentrated in and

44. Ibid., 76–77.
45. Ibid., 171.

originates from the direction of those who resist almost all government standards.[46]

Two days later (August 20), Susan Berry answered "from the political and ideological Right" with a response op-ed entitled, "*NY Times*' Keller Tries and Fails to Defend Common Core."[47] Berry's response to Keller also followed a blog entry from Diane Ravitch on August 19, wherein Ravitch quotes and endorses Susan Ohanian's critique of Keller "from the 'left.'"[48] Ohanian adopts an angle of debate not unlike Gatto's, wherein she notes that the rights to Common Core curriculum publications have been purchased and retained for twenty years by a Rupert Murdoch–owned company, Amplify.

These were followed on August 21, by Charles Blow's op-ed, contributing his own point of view to the debate: "The Common Core and the Common Good." With almost graceful finesse, Blow unreservedly endorses the need for and the concept and direction of common core, while naming the obvious potholes in various attempts to implement common core programmatically. Among such potholes are: (a) Top-down implementation efforts prior to achieving adequate constituency training, orientation, and buy-in; and (b) "prioritizing testing over teaching," and therefore "punishment over preparation." He then names four supplemental, yet essential, needs: teacher quality-development and retention; "providing 'wrap around' services for poor and struggling students;" making schools that offer education and services that stakeholders sense are safe, welcoming, inspiring, fun, nurturing, and nutritious; and establishing "learning to think critically and to solve problems" as the number one priority. Blow concludes by returning to his supplemental need, that for "great teachers" who develop among students intellectual curiosity, perseverance, and an expansive capacity and thirst for learning. Blow believes that common core standards and efforts with these complementary factors being

46. Keller, "War on the Core."

47. Berry, "*NY Times*' Keller Tries and Fails to Defend Common Core."

48 Ravitch, "The *New York Times* Hearts Common Core: Susan Ohanian Calls Foul."

recognized and achieved is the way to go. He concludes with the conviction, "The Common Core is for the common good, if only we can get our act together and properly implement it."[49]

This is not saying that Hirsch and his associates are wrong in advancing their perspective on core knowledge in learning. It is worth remembering continually, though, that among education professionals and parents, a variety of concerns from several angles exist in relation to learning and education content and goals. Blow seems to recognize and articulate the multiple factors, influences, and challenges better than most in these debates.

Like Charles Blow in ability to identify and address challenges that are chronic, subtle, and severe, Gloria Ladson-Billings moves this discussion with a progressive nudge that does not completely abandon Hirsch's goal, yet that also takes Postman's "narratives" and "stories of humanity" several steps forward. She contributes immeasurably to this topic and debate with specific explorations, observations, and applications to "majority racial-ethnic" communities and schools.

In *The Dream-Keepers: Successful Teachers of African American Children*, Ladson-Billings writes: "I began his book with a question: Do African American students need separate schools? I conclude with an answer: What African American students need are better schools. I contend that culturally relevant teaching practices would be an integral part of these schools." She outlines six objectives which she is convinced, when adopted and implemented, over time will make important improvements in teaching quality, effectiveness, and results. The six are:

> (a) Recruit teacher candidates who have expressed an interest and a desire to work with African American students; (b) provide educational experiences that help teachers understand the central role of culture; (c) provide teacher candidates with opportunities to critique the system (in their teaching with their students) in ways that will help the students choose a role as either agent of change or defender of the status quo; (d) systematically

49. Blow, "The Common Core and the Common Good."

require teacher candidates to have prolonged immersion in African American culture; (e) provide opportunities for observation of culturally relevant teaching; (f) conduct student teaching over a longer period of time and in a more controlled environment.[50]

Following her declaration of objectives for effective teachers in schools mostly populated with African American students, she describes three components evident through a culturally relevant school: "(a) provides educational self-determination; (b) honors and respects the student's home culture; and (c) helps African American students understand the world as it is and equip them to change it for the better."[51]

The corrective Ladson-Billings and Postman offer to Hirsch and others (who focus on core knowledge mastery to the exclusion—largely—of contingent contextual variables and factors) seems to be an essential one. The potential benefit of their corrective is rooted in an unapologetic appreciation for diversity in areas of life that include economic, ethnic, and racial variations, multiple cultural contexts and traditions, and special needs.

10. The person, "It," is asked: "Is 'social Darwinism' involved as a positive or an incentivist element?"

Answer for the game of Eleven Questions: "Only in a qualified way."

One goal of a positive education for the common good might ironically be characterized as including and advocating the studying, pondering, researching, and debating of Charles Darwin's scientific findings and hypotheses, while seeking to go beyond certain implications of "social Darwinism."

Darwin published *Origin of the Species* (1859) and *The Descent of Man* (1871). Some have thought that his theory of the survival of the fittest carries over easily and consistently to a sociological description known as "social Darwinism," asserting that, within human groupings and categorical classifications and associations, the

50. Ladson-Billings, *The Dreamkeepers*, 225, 143–48.

51. Ibid., 150–53.

fittest adapt to threats and changes and survive, evolving over generations, while the inferior individuals and groups go by the wayside.

Not everyone buys into social Darwinism; yet the arguments related to category-analyses that bear Darwin's name need to be examined in their distinctive constituent parts. Moreover, while it may not seem self-evident or obvious to someone who has never considered this perspective, this question and assessment may be as important, or more important, than any other. It is essential.

One can identify at least four rather distinct camps or perspectives in this assessment.

a. Religiously fundamental persons, or, phrased differently, literalists who, whether they be Christian, Jewish, Muslim, or some other faith, promote a perspective that clearly opposes Darwin's scientific hypotheses related to the evolutionary developments of species. These prefer an understanding that God creates identifiably distinct species without any primitive evolutionary development. Such "anti-Darwinists," biologically speaking, however, give ample evidence of inconsistency, due to their human-sociological practices of competitive instincts and inclinations. They are often not hesitant about advancing their own strength and numbers while seeking policy victories that minimize or vanquish those whom they consider rivals. They oppose Darwin's hypotheses related to biology, while socially and politically practicing survival of the fittest unapologetically and sometimes with a vengeance.

Although many religious persons fully realize that education in the subjects of science does not methodologically include religious narratives and teachings, frequently anti-Darwinists argue that their worry is a fear of being oppressed, and perhaps of being vanquished, by a wave of scientific secularism that (they believe) intrudes on and assaults their constitutionally protected freedom to hold and practice their religious values (they would say) even in public school classrooms.

b. Another camp or perspective related to education promotes Darwin's biological hypotheses scientifically and practices survival of the fittest in relation to other groups' educational, religious, ethnic, or economic "rival perspectives," whether this is necessarily declared as part of their vision or goals statements, or not. Among education specialists, many empiricists might be counted among this group, broadly speaking: those who practice high-stakes testing and evaluations; those who elevate the successful students and professionals without equal attention to and regard for those not as successfully exceptional; those who seek to minimize public or personal relationships with others whose perspectives or life contexts vary from their own, either somewhat or substantially.

In this particular characterization, related to survival of the fittest, practitioners and "embracers" can be either conservative or liberal, conscious and intentional in their convictions and relationships, or unconscious and unintentional. For all of us as human beings, regardless of our particular perspectives, beliefs, and orientations, there's the strong temptation to leave behind those whom we consider to be substantially different, because they are outside of our comfort zone, and to leave behind the severely challenged because they cannot keep up, and the energy drain of nurturing and including both groups is ongoing. (Saying this does not excuse such behavior and outcomes, it's rather an essential acknowledgement and confession.)

c. John Gatto articulates an historical, analytical narrative establishing a third perspective that can be neutral toward Darwin's biological biological and scientific hypotheses, yet which identifies (as adversarial and oppositional) the imposition of stress as a biological and sociological element. He writes: "Evolutionary socialists were taught by [Friedrich] Hegel to see struggle as the precipitant of evolutionary improvement for the species, a necessary purifier eliminating the weak from the breeding sweepstakes. Society evolves slowly toward 'social efficiency' all by itself; society under stress, however, evolves much faster! Thus the deliberate creation of crisis is an important tool of evolutionary socialists." Immediately preceding this statement, Gatto writes: "[There is] nothing illegal about it. I do think it a tragedy, however, that government school children are left in the dark about the existence of influential groups with complex social agendas aimed at their lives."[52]

Gatto advocates education as liberated as possible from government and bureaucratic control, wherein students might experience a learning environment free from the stress of systems that regiment processes, institutionalize learning, and create categorical divisions based upon and leading to success-and-failure determinations. He writes: "By the end of World War I, the familiar Common School idea survived only in the imagination of America's middle and working class. In actual school practice, [the Common School idea] had given way to thoroughly regulated and tracked assemblages geared tightly to the clock, managed by layered hierarchies and all schematized into rigid class rankings. Class-reproduction was 'scientifically' locked in place by standardized test scores, calibrated to the decimal . . ."[53]

In summary, to this point: While group (a) resists and opposes Darwinian hypotheses in biology, arguably they practice forms of social Darwinism in their political relationships and policy advocacy when faced with opposition that they sense needs to be diminished or eliminated. Group (b) accepts and promotes Darwinian hypotheses in understanding and teaching of biology, and other sciences, and they often practice social

52. Gatto, *Underground*, 183
53. Ibid., 350.

Darwinism when instituting policies and articulating and implementing vision statements and the attendant policies related to them. Group (c) can be neutral on the biological aspects of Darwinism but opposes any imposition of stress for students' success in the process of education, which is opposition to stress both in theory and in practice.

d. The fourth group is instructed by and generally accepts the validity of Darwinian implications, both in biology and in sociology; yet these folk seek to ferret out and to counterbalance the natural selection/ fittest survival arc with systems mediated by legislation, public policy, and diligent personal and corporate efforts, in pursuit of goals that are characterized by seeking and striving toward public education for the common good, while making allowances and concessions for special needs.

So, is social Darwinism involved as a positive, or incentivist element? It likely cannot be labeled positive, as such; neither should there be policy and practice incentives leading to advantages for the success of some and reducing success possibilities for others. Yet I disagree with Gatto, suspecting that stress can be helpful, when well managed. Appropriate performance efforts (which may include degrees of stress) can contribute to shared success by individuals and groups and can be positive for prompting and encouraging persons and communities to improved policies, relationships, results, learning, and greater wholeness as human beings. This is possible even with no end in sight, since public education, like education in general, and like the future itself, is on a continuum, never fixed, and is still evolving.

11. With these ten questions asked and answered with comments, the eleventh question (we hope) could be: "Is the subject-answer for today's game, 'A positive public education for the common good?'" And the answer to this eleventh question (we hope) is, "Yes!"

Toward this end, whether persons espouse and are fed by values for the common good that have either religious sources and roots or philosophically secular sources and roots, crucial partnerships and alliances, collaborations and compromises are possible and necessary in the shared sacred calling that is public education.

Epilogue and Afterword

My steps along the road of exploring and investigating this theme have been prompted by at least the seven quotes that here follow. Three are from persons or characters of whom I have read. Four are from persons who have shared their insights, multiple gifts, and passionate caring one-on-one with me at some point in my own life.

> 1. "We are terrified that if once we allow ourselves to be cracked—I think people really do think that they're eggs . . . [and we] have a 'Humpty Dumpty' complex . . ."
> —character Matt Friedman, in Lanford Wilson's *Talley's Folly*[1]

Through his character, Matt Friedman, playwright Lanford Wilson articulates how personal brokenness is a characteristic that thrills none of us; and we feel similarly about brokenness in society, on a scale beyond each individual. We, therefore, prefer to ignore the possibility of brokenness altogether; yet we are all already "cracked" all the time. We are already cracked, and "all the King's horses and all the King's men" simply do not exist—and are not capable even if they did exist—to come galloping in to put us back together again. We are, in life, however, given each other, along with the possibility of moving together beyond our respective states of "cracked-ness," given how we are public stakeholders with diverse and varied gifts for contributing to the common good.

1. Wilson, *Talley's Folly*, 49.

2. "Let's gather round mentally." —Dr. Ralph L. Lynn
(1909–2007; Professor of History, Baylor University)

Dr. Ralph Lynn was an expert at bringing the past alive in his European history classrooms and in his life-stewardship beyond the classroom, always pursuing the common good. Any time Dr. Lynn challenged, encouraged, or advocated for one individual, his challenges, encouragements, and advocacy were neither random nor unconnected from others. His challenging, encouraging, and advocating for any one individual were always offered with a view toward the importance of the connection all have with each other one. The study of history, Dr. Lynn was convinced, assists our discovery of starting points in order to understand and engage societal challenges of both past and present. Whether leading or participating in a classroom lecture, a graduate level seminar, or a group project out among communities beyond academia, Dr. Lynn believed that we all do best when the invitation to "gather round mentally" is genuinely and enthusiastically declared.

> 3. "Democracy is not an end, but the best means for achieving the values of equality, justice, freedom, peace, a deep concern for the lives of all persons as taught in Judeo-Christianity and the democratic tradition. The basic requirement for understanding the politics of change is to recognize the world as-it-is in order to change it to the kind of world we would like for it to be." —Saul D. Alinsky (1909–72)[2]

These sentences from Saul Alinsky's *Rules for Radicals: A Pragmatic Primer for Realistic Radicals* might say all that needs to be said about the healthiest intersection possible of political philosophy, history, religion, and real life with human beings in community.

> 4. "Can you tell the class who is your hero today, and defend your answer?"—Lloyd Mitchell (1907–91; eleventh-grade American history teacher, Gatesville, Texas)

---

2. Alinsky, *Rules for Radicals*, 12.

Weekday after weekday for decades, Coach Mitchell began his classes with this invitation for students to contribute to a community dialog based on their reading and comprehension of current events and potentially admirable contributions to the common good by persons widely known and persons hardly known. As an adult thinking back across the succeeding years and chapters of my life, I now believe that Coach Mitchell was likely asking students to determine heroes in a way similar to Tolstoy's method: The widowed homemaker or sharecropper in the remote village contributes to history; the Czar of Russia contributes to history; there are distinctions in the ways and the ripple-effects of their contributions, yet both are citizen-stakeholders, and both are potential contributors and potential heroes for the common good.

> 5. "Students, today is a red-letter grade day!" —Fay Shurtleff Eubanks (1902–88; seventh-grade English teacher, Gatesville, Texas)

Ms. Eubanks' teaching methods in the literature sections of the curriculum she taught substantially employed: memory lines from sections of poetry and prose; and discussion and written assignments for expressing understanding and critiquing what was memorized. Such days of recitation and analysis, she enthusiastically declared, were "red-letter-grade days." As years have passed, I've grown to sense that every day is a day not to be wasted, but, as each day is given with time, each day includes opportunities for contributing to the common good. Every day is a red-letter-grade day, or a day to prepare for the red-letter-grade days yet to come.

> 6. "If I could wish one thing for you . . . it's a passion . . . that will go the distance." —character Scottie Templeton, in Bernard Slade's *Tribute*[3]

Arguably, we all need what character Scottie Templeton wishes for his young adult son, Jud. A complicating factor, however, in Bernard Slade's *Tribute* and in real life, is how Scottie and many of us sometimes so overshadow others that the others encounter

3. Slade, *Tribute*, 89.

difficulty in the way their passion might find space or daylight to grow and develop. Scottie's wish expressed for his son is surely our wish for all stakeholders in the common good. Truly, learning through life the best methods and the abiding respect and patience each of us can practice so that others have space and daylight to experience, develop, and own their passion is a worthy goal for each and every one of us, all the time.

> 7. "Let's do it!" —Erin Channing Buenger (1997–2009;
> student, Mary Branch Middle School, Bryan, Texas)

Erin Buenger's life was abbreviated in years due to neuroblastoma, yet hers was also a life characterized by collaboration, commitment for the common good, love that was both public and personal, and energy only slowed by that malignant virus that one day stopped her breathing but not her influence. Once an idea grew into a constructive plan, Erin pronounced a verdict and gave the verbal signal: "Let's do it." No challenge, she believed, was insurmountable.

In the relay race that is life and history, batons, in due season, are always being handed off to others. The key is awareness of need, collaboration for discerning and assessing the common good, pursuing worthy goals as diverse partners, and then reassessing for the next advance.

Erin became determined that pediatric cancer research should never take a backseat to research focused on any other forms of cancer, and that no class of patients (children, for example) should have dated treatment resources because research (and funding for research) had lagged.[4] Isn't that a paradigm we legitimately affirm and understand in public education? No student should have educational limitations because the public system responsible for the common good deferred, transferred, slackened, or abdicated crucial efforts. The only acceptable alternative is for us to heed Erin's admonition: "Let's do it" as public stakeholders, every day.

While I am instructed and inspired by voices like these from my past, I conclude this effort with the same confession with

---

4. Phelps, "Girl Lobbying for Funding to Fight Cancer."

which I began chapter 1: "I am an outsider" (in relation to the vast depth and breadth of both education and public education, especially in a professional sense). This confession—with humility and trepidation—reminds us that a legitimate component of every person's approach to life on a daily basis is knowing what you don't know. From that point forward—all the time—one is surely able to hear inwardly the whisper of Alexander Pope's hauntingly accurate observation from 1709: "Fools rush in where angels fear to tread."[5]

We need not be intimidated by this on-target assessment. Rather, we can be made humble and helpfully confident that collaborative and complementary contributions to the common good by a diverse body of citizen-stakeholders are possible. If we go forward respectfully, openly, hopefully, inquiringly, and boldly, expecting to learn and become wiser together, our learning and becoming wiser together will happen, even though only some are professional educators. We may not learn and become wiser together in the ways we could have guessed in advance along the journey, but learning and becoming wiser together will occur, because life itself and public education as part of life are both larger than any of us.

Cracked eggs that we are, in Erin Buenger's words, "Let's do it!"

---

5. Pope, *An Essay on Criticism* (Part III).

Appendix A

Developing a Compatible Rationale for Public Ethics and Cooperative Service among Both Religious and Non-Religious Persons

THERE ARE AS MANY perspectives on biblical and religious interpretations as there are persons, because no two persons hold and practice identical biblical and religious interpretations.

This appendix is provided in an effort to facilitate, for those who may be interested, a brief consideration of a working biblical and religious interpretation method: not one that will be identical from one person to another, but rather one that will offer a way forward or methodology characterized by clarity and simplicity, without oversimplifying or stereotyping.

The table below indicates, at its top, a binary, polarized perspective that positions religious values on one side and secular values on the other.

Appendix A

Religious Values		Secular Values
	OR	
nonsectarian		secular
comprehensive		non-exclusive
stewardship/ serving	combining with	education/ issues
		approaches

This is not meant to indicate authoritatively that one is holy and its opposite is profane. That sort of thinking has too often led to conflicts in personal or community and public relationships, and has yielded more manifestations of pain, trauma, suffering, division, and alienation than ever should be created, advanced, or perpetuated in any form.

This pairing of religious values opposite secular values is, rather, a recognition that some people are convinced that many persons' respective religious traditions—concerning what is considered true and sacred and how those values are held, practiced, and treasured—becomes the polar opposite of secularists who have no such religious values.

This certainly may be the case: that the two groups have few or no values in common. It may be the case, but it might not be an air-tight exclusivism.

The United States Constitution forbids the establishment of a religion or, phrased differently, forbids practices that imply establishment of one or more religious traditions that may seem to coerce conformity to any particular religious tradition or set of practices, as much as it means particular religious traditions will be allowed to practice the observances of their respective tradition without government's overreach and interference. Some have labeled this, variously, as "freedom from religion" or "freedom for religion."

Religious persons and groups considered sectarian are those who demand of others near-absolute conformity to their own religious expressions and beliefs before accepting those others as valid, only affirming as acceptable the truly "converted." Nonsectarian religious persons of any religious tradition, however, may:

(1) recognize validity "under God and from God" among religious traditions different from their own; and (2) recognize validity among "the secular" who respectfully acknowledge that others who hold religious traditions that are not exclusivistic may share common ground with them (secularists) on certain values.

If the secularist's perspective and practice is something other than greed or selfishness, then certain nonreligious or secularist persons might hold values that are similar to (or almost identical with) nonsectarian religious persons. This certainly could be the situation if the nonsectarian religious persons hold, at the heart of their faith, the crucial importance of being stewards of God's gifts throughout creation, during each one's life span, and trans-generationally.

While nonsectarian religious persons can say they "are 'called' by God to a life and vocation of being stewards of God's gifts with utmost care, gratitude, and celebration for those gifts," the only difference a secular (or nonreligious) person might have with such a life approach and interaction with public education are the words "God" and "God's."

So nonsectarian religious persons who believe it is important to build cooperative alliances and avenues of common service for the common good have common ground to serve with secularists who are willing to cooperate with nonsectarian religious persons, provided the secularists also believe in the high purpose of being stewards of the resources of creation and humanity all through each person's life and across generations.

Nonsectarian religious persons who understand themselves as having received a calling or vocation from God to be serving, for example—as Christians would say, "in the way and spirit of Jesus"—might, beyond a label of "Christian" and with a practice of comprehensive and positive neighborliness in relation to all others as siblings in the family of God, look to passages of the following chapters and verses of the Jewish and Christian scriptures for guidance and encouragement in ways of serving God faithfully.

a. Deuteronomy 6:5; Loving God with all of one's being in life

b. Leviticus 19:18; Loving one's neighbor as one's self

c. Amos 5:14–15, 23–24; Establishing equity and justice among the public, as God desires

d. Micah 6:8; Working for justice, exhibiting faithful loving-kindness, and living with humility before God, as God desires

e. Jeremiah 29:1, 4–14; Seeking the well-being of the community where one lives, because in seeking the community's well-being, we find our own well-being also

f. Matthew 22:34–40; Mark 12:24–34; Luke 10:25–37; Jesus endorsing Deuteronomy 6:5 and Leviticus 19:18. (cf. "a" and "b" of this list of examples)

g. Luke 18:18–23; Jesus encouraging a wealthy person to share generously in behalf of the poor and economically deprived

h. Luke 20:19–26; Jesus encouraging public participation in citizen responsibilities which do not conflict with a faith relationship with God

i. John 21:15–19; Jesus encouraging love from his followers to be shared and lived out among God's people

j. Acts 10:27–29, 34–35; 11:9, 17–18; Followers of Jesus learning how God is at work to lead them to accept others outside of their fellowship as being people of God in God's family who are equal with them, no matter to what degree and with what line of thinking they have previously thought God actually excludes those who are different

k. James 1:22; 2:14–26; Encouragement for persons who profess to be Christian to serve others with actions that are caring, helping, and empowering, and that match the words that are spoken related to religious faith

l. I John 4:16–21; A teaching that love is practiced fearlessly in life relationships because God is the essence and source of the love people are given and called to practice.

Especially worthy of consideration in the list above is item (e), Jeremiah 29, verses 7 and 11, with the admonitions from God (through Jeremiah's prophetic letter) to the former citizens of Jerusalem who had been carried into exile in Babylon by the conquering army of Babylon. God, through Jeremiah, exhorts the community of the faithful there to "seek the well-being (Hebrew *shalom*) of the city where you are, because, in its well-being will be your well-being."

This is arguably the function of the public in public education, both in the understanding of the religiously faithful who already are nonsectarian, and in the potential understanding of religious sectarians who hear the pleading of God to be engaged in a broader vision of God's *shalom*-seeking with every person in the diverse communities where we live. Those secularists (who are not excluders of nonsectarian religious persons) surely can find willing allies in and with the nonsectarian religious as both seek the common good and the well-being of our communities—during the present and into the future—in the endeavor and enterprise that is public education.

Appendix B

Qualitative Interview Process and Demographics

THE QUALITATIVE RESEARCH ASPECT of this project consisted of (1) twenty-one replies on a questionnaire submitted to a variety of classroom teachers and administrators, and (2) forty-one personal interviews of (a) classroom teachers and administrators, in addition to (b) persons who were related to education in ways different from classroom instruction and administration. All participants were assured that their participation in the survey or the interview would be protected as confidential.

The questionnaires were sent to persons whom I knew previously or whom I had hoped to interview personally and discovered this was not possible. Those who completed the written questionnaires lived in Texas, Oklahoma, and California. The questionnaire asked for responses to questions related to: (a) persons influential in the educators' life who helped lead them to their vocational and occupational choice of this profession; (b) their greatest sense of fulfillment; (c) their greatest frustrations; (d) what they would change in education if they had a magic wand to effect such change immediately; and (e) what has fueled the degree of passion they feel for the enterprise, endeavor, and journey of education involvement.

The questions on the written request for participation in the project were the same questions that kick-started the personal interviews; yet the personal interviews included aspects and dimensions of responses not possible or available in a written reply to questions. The interviews varied in length from thirty minutes to sixty-five minutes and were digitally recorded for my review and accuracy in recalling.

Both types of inquiries served the same purpose: To help me, as an outsider, become acquainted with the world of education, and particularly public education. Prior to the interviews, I had done cursory reading and research to acquaint myself with what are generally considered to be issues related to United States education history, twenty-first century education vision and goals, public education policy, and administration roles locally, regionally, and nationally. Following the interviews, I entered the reading-intensive phase of the project.

The interviews mostly are not reproduced in the manuscript. The reality at the end of the project differs from my anticipation prior to embarking on the writing itself. I discovered that I doubted my ability adequately to portray the richness of the interviews (yes, the written ones, but more the face-to-face interviews) in ways that would seem more than anecdotal.

The task of producing a primer is to describe issues and perspectives through a broad or panoramic treatment. I, therefore, relied on the surveys and interviews to be the unseen accuracy check (although subjective) to what I read, initially in cursory fashion, and later intensively.

The personal interviews were conducted during five trips to different parts of the United States, which included eight states and the District of Columbia: in the Mid-Atlantic, Midwest, Deep South, Southwest, and the southwestern Pacific Coast. Of the forty-one interviews, the classifications of settings and persons are as follows.

Settings: (a) urban—22; (b) suburban—2; (c) medium-sized/small city (less than 150,000)—4; (d) "county-seat"/rural—13.

Racial/ethnic background of interviewees: (a) African American—6; (b) Hispanic—3; (c) Caucasian—32.

Gender: (a) male—18; (b) female—23.

Public education roles/involvement: classroom educators, (a) pre-kindergarten through fifth/sixth grades—9; (b) sixth/seventh through eighth/ninth grades—3; ninth/tenth through twelfth grade—8; (d) principals—5; (e) superintendents—4; (f) vocational school educators (beyond high school)—2; (g) custodian—1; (h) parents—4; (i) school board member, education program administrator, education consultant, legislator, citizens' group advocate—5.

This sample, even when the twenty-one written responses are added, is obviously miniscule when compared to the number of persons involved in United States public education. It is selective and random to the extent that I had never met any of the interviewees before being referred to them from someone whom I knew or before I found them through an Internet search and subsequent request. For the purposes of this primer, these samples are limited, and, strictly speaking, as research, are limiting. In my judgment, however, they have been incomparably informative, essential, and enriching.

Appendix C

Outline Diagram for Chapter 6,
Varied Education Trajectories

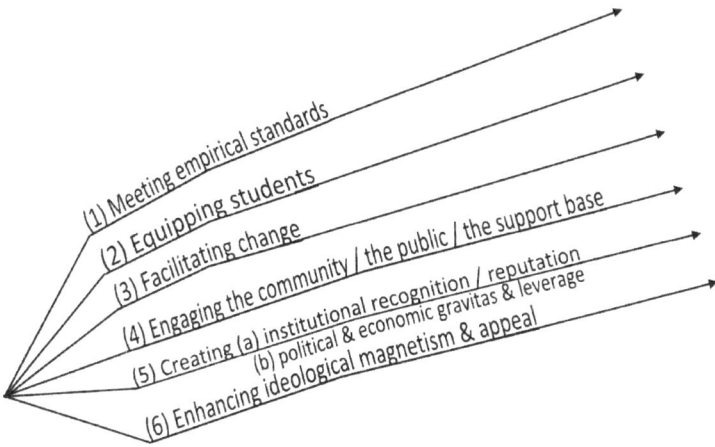

(1) Meeting empirical standards

(2) Equipping students

(3) Facilitating change

(4) Engaging the community / the public / the support base

(5) Creating (a) institutional recognition / reputation
(b) political & economic gravitas & leverage

(6) Enhancing ideological magnetism & appeal

Appendix D

Outline Diagram for Chapter 7, Approach-Perspectives to Twelve Challenge Topics

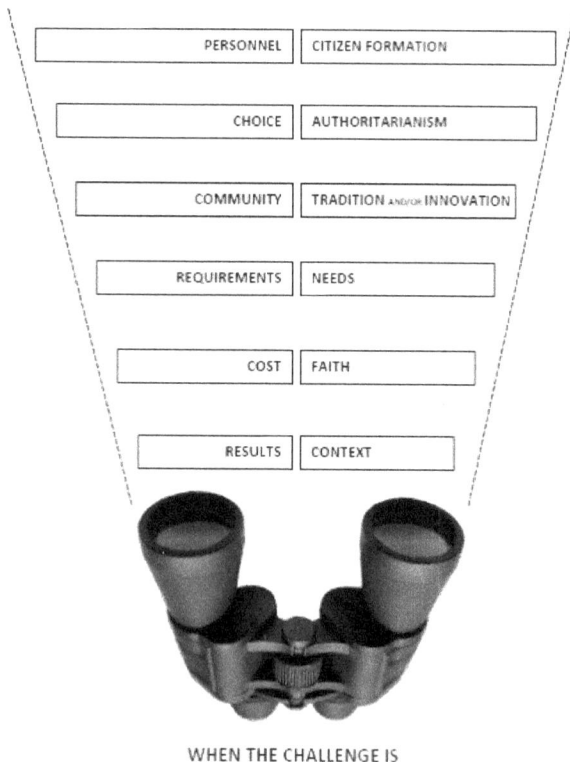

PERSONNEL	CITIZEN FORMATION
CHOICE	AUTHORITARIANISM
COMMUNITY	TRADITION and/or INNOVATION
REQUIREMENTS	NEEDS
COST	FAITH
RESULTS	CONTEXT

WHEN THE CHALLENGE IS

Appendix E

List of Questions for Chapter 8, Eleven Questions Related to Public Education for the Common Good

1. (Question) Is ideology involved?
   (Answer) Yes.

2. (Q) If destructive stress exists where ideology is present, is the ideology (or, are the ideologies) involved a virus or a vitamin?"
   (A) Virus.

3. (Q) Are teachers and their collective voices involved?
   (A) Yes.

4. (Q) Are teachers and classroom educators—individually and collectively—best understood as solution inhibitors or as solution contributors?
   (A) Solution contributors.

5. (Q) Are high-stakes testing, teacher-effectiveness evaluations, and results-driven philosophies involved?
   (A) They can be.

6. (Q) Are high-stakes testing, teacher-effectiveness evaluations, and results-driven philosophies involved as the primary means for overcoming students' low achievement and
   enhancing the nation's future?
   (A) No.

7. (Q) Are school choice and select schools necessarily involved
   in this endeavor?
   (A) No. Not necessarily. Certainly not exclusively.

8. (Q) Is more public funding involved?
   (A) Likely always.

9. (Q) Are challenging factors of diversity—for example, economic, ethnic, racial variation; multiple cultural contexts and
   traditions; special needs, etc.—negative or positive?
   (A) Positive.

10. (Q) Is "social Darwinism" involved as a positive or an incen-
    tivist element?
    (A)Only in a qualified way.

11. Concluding question from the ten previous:
    (Q) Might this endeavor or enterprise be "a positive public
    education for the common good?"
    (A) Yes.

Bibliography

American Academy of Arts and Sciences. "The Heart of the Matter: The Humanities and Social Sciences for a Vibrant, Competitive, Secure Nation." Cambridge, MA, 2013. https://www.amacad.org/content/publications/publication.aspx?d=21724.

Alinsky, Saul D. Rules for Radicals: A Pragmatic Primer for Realistic Radicals. New York: Vintage, 1971.

Ayers, William. To Teach: The Journey of a Teacher. New York: Teachers' College Press, 2001.

Barzun, Jacques. The Culture We Deserve. Middletown, CT: Wesleyan University Press, 1989.

———. Teacher in America. Boston: Little, Brown and Co., 1945.

Bellah, Robert N., et al. Habits of the Heart: Individualism and Commitment in American Life. New York: Harper and Row, 1985.

Berlin, Isaiah. The Proper Study of Mankind: An Anthology of Essays. New York: Farrar, Straus, and Giroux, 1997.

Berry, Susan. "NY Times' Keller Tries and Fails to Defend Common Core." http://www.breitbart.com/Big-Journalism/2013/08/19/NYT-Defends-Common-Core-Standards.

Bettis-Gee, Martha. "Public Education: Right or Privilege?" The Thoughtful Christian (2011). www.TheThoughtfulChristian.com.

Binder, Amy J. Contentious Curricula: Afrocentrism and Creationism in American Public Schools. Princeton: Princeton University Press, 2002.

Blow, Charles M. "The Common Core and the Common Good." New York Times, August 21, 2013. http://www.nytimes.com/2013/08/22/opinion/blow-the-common-core-and-the-common-good.html?_r=0.

Brimelow, Peter. The Worm in the Apple: How the Teacher Unions Are Destroying American Education. New York: Perennial/Harper Collins, 2003.

Brueggemann, Walter. Journey to the Common Good. Louisville, KY: Westminster/John Knox, 2010.

Butts, R. Freeman. Public Education in the United States: From Revolution to Reform. New York: Holt, Rinehart, and Winston, 1978.

Cahill, Thomas. How the Irish Saved Civilization: The Untold Story of Ireland's Heroic Role from the Fall of Rome to the Rise of Medieval Europe. New York: Doubleday, 1995.

Cobb, John B., Jr. Postmodernism and Public Policy: Reframing Religion, Culture, Education, Sexuality, Class, Race, Politics, and the Economy Albany, New York: State University of New York Press, 2002.

Cobb, John B. Jr. Reclaiming the Church: Where the Mainline Church Went Wrong and What to Do about It. Louisville, KY: Westminster/John Knox, 1997.

Cohen, Brad, and Lisa Wysocky. Front of the Class: How Tourette Syndrome Made Me the Teacher I Never Had. New York: St. Martin's Griffin, 2005, 2008.

Collins, Gail. As Texas Goes: How the Lone Star State Hijacked the American Agenda. New York: W. W. Norton, 2012.

Corneliussen, Steven T. "High-Stakes Testing: David Brooks vs. Diane Ravitch." Physics Today (July 11, 2011). http://www.physicstoday.org/daily_edition/science_and_the_media/1.2559466

Covey, Stephen R. The Seven Habits of Highly Effective People: Powerful Lessons in Personal Change. New York: Simon & Schuster/Free Press, 1989/2004.

Dewey, John. Democracy and Education Rochester, NY: MacMillan, 1916.

————. The Influence of Darwin on Philosophy and Other Essays in Contemporary Thought. New York: Peter Smith, 1951.

————. The Public and Its Problems Athens, OH: Swallow Press, 1927, 1954 [re-issue].

Dowd, Michael. Thank God for Evolution: How the Marriage of Science and Religion Will Transform Your Life and Our World. NY: Penguin, 2007.

Elmore, Richard F., ed. I Used to Think . . . And Now I Think . . .:Twenty Leading Educators Reflect on the Work of School Reform. Cambridge, MA: Harvard University Press, 2011.

Esquith, Rafe. Lighting Their Fires: Raising Extraordinary Children in a Mixed-up, Muddled-up, Shook-up World. New York: Viking/Penguin, 2009.

————. Real Talk for Real Teachers: Advice for Teachers from Rookies to Veterans—"No Retreat, No Surrender!" New York: Viking/Penguin, 2013.

————. Teach Like Your Hair's on Fire: The Methods and Madness Inside Room 56 New York: Penguin, 2007.

Farley, Edward. Practicing Gospel: Unconventional Thoughts on the Church's Ministry Louisville, KY: Westminster/John Knox, 2003.

Farr, Steven, Wendy Kopp, and Jason Kamras. Teaching as Leadership: The Highly Effective guide to Closing the Achievement Gap. San Francisco: Jossey-Bass, 2010.

Fulgham, Nicole Baker. Educating All God's Children: What Christians Can—and Should—Do to Improve Public Education for Low-Income Kids. Grand Rapids: Brazos, 2013.

————. "Beyond 'Superman:' Four Traits of Successful Public School Reform." Sojourners (September–October 2012) 20–23.

Gatto, John Taylor. Dumbing Us Down: The Hidden Curriculum of Compulsory Schooling. Gabriola Island, BC: New Society, 1992/2005.

————. The Underground History of American Education: An Intimate Investigation into the Prison of Modern Schooling. New York: Oxford Village, 2006.

Goldstein, Dana. The Teacher Wars: A History of America's Most Embattled Profession New York: Doubleday, 2014.

Green, Charles Leslie Jr. The Myth of the Common School. Amherst, MA: University of Massachusetts Press, 1988.

Gruwell, Erin. The Freedom Writers Diary. New York: Broadway/Random House, 1999.

————. Teach With Your Heart: Lessons I Learned from the Freedom Writers. New York: Broadway/Random House, 2007.

————, ed. Teaching Hope: Stories from The Freedom Writer Teachers. New York: Broadway/Random House, 2009.

Herman, Arthur. How the Scots Invented the Modern World. New York: Three Rivers, 2001.

Hirsch, E. D. Jr. The Schools We Need and Why We Don't Have Them. New York: Anchor/Random House, 1996.

Keillor, Garrison. A Prairie Home Companion. National Public Radio, February 2, 2015.

Keller, Bill. "War on the Core." New York Times, August 18, 2013. http://www.nytimes.com/2013/08/19/opinion/keller-war-on-the-core.html?pagewanted=all.

Kennedy, Kelli. "Teen Pregnancy Study: Students Need Better School Support." Huffington Post, November 22, 2012. http://www.huffingtonpost.com/2012/11/24/teen-pregnancy-study-stud_n_2185062.html

Klein, Joel, and Condoleezza Rice. "U.S. Education Reform and National Security." Council on Foreign Relations. March 2012. http://www.cfr.org/united-states/us-education-reform-national-security/p27618.

Kozol, Jonathan. Letters to a Young Teacher. New York: Crown/Random House, 2007.

————. Savage Inequalities: Children in America's Schools. New York: HarperCollins Crown/Perennial, 1991, 1992.

Ladson-Billings, Gloria, ed. Critical Race Theory Perspectives on the Social Studies: The Profession, Policies, and Curriculum. Greenwich, CT: Information Age Publishing, 2003.

————. The Dreamkeepers: Successful Teachers of African-American Children. San Francisco: Jossey-Bass, 2009.

Lisee, Chris. "Air Force Academy Proselytizing and Religious Freedom Debate on School Campus." Religious News Service, July 17, 2012. http://www.huffingtonpost.com/2012/07/17/air-force-academy-religion-proselytism_n_1678092.html.

Marty, Martin E. The Public Church: Mainline—Evangelical—Catholic. New York: Crossroad, 1981.

Mathews, David. Reclaiming Public Education by Reclaiming Our Democracy. Dayton, OH: Kettering Foundation, 2006.

———. "The Public and the Public Schools: The Coproduction of Education." Phi Delta Kappan, April 2008. 560–64. http://www.kappanmagazine.org/content/89/8/560.abstract.

McCleskey, Bob. "School of Thought: Funding Decision Victory for Equality." Arkansas Democrat-Gazette, December 10, 2012. http:www.arkansasonline.com/news/2012/dec/10/school-thought-20121210/.

Milliken, Bill. The Last Dropout: Stop the Epidemic. Carlsbad, CA: Hay House, 2007.

Mondale, Sarah, and Sarah B. Patton. School: the Story of American Public Education Boston: Beacon, 2001.

Moulthrop, Daniel, Ninive Clements Calegari, and Dave Eggers. Teachers Have It Easy: The Big Sacrifices and Small Salaries of America's Teachers. New York: The New Press, 2005.

Mudge, Lewis S. The Sense of a People: Toward a Church for the Human Future. Philadelphia: Trinity Press International, 1992.

Nutter, Michael, and Chris Hayes. "All In With Chris Hayes." MSNBC, June 10, 2013. http://www.nbcnews.com/id/52168305/ns/msnbc-all_in_with_chris_hayes/t/all-chris-hayes-monday-june-th/.

Ogden, Dunbar H. My Father Said Yes: A White Pastor in Little Rock School Integration Nashville: Vanderbilt University Press, 2008.

Osgood, Katie. "Paul Tough Is Way Off-Base. And Stop Saying 'Grit.'" http://atthechalkface.com/2012/09/30/paul-tough-is-way-off-base-and-stop-saying-grit/.

Palmer, Parker J. The Courage To Teach: Exploring the Inner Landscape of a Teacher's Life. San Francisco: Jossey-Bass, 1998/2007.

———. To Know As We Are Known: Education as a Spiritual Journey. San Francisco: Harper/Collins, 1983/1993.

Patterson, Orlando, Freedom: Vol. I, Freedom in the Making of Western Culture. New York: Basic Books/Perseus, 1991.

Percy, Walker. Love in the Ruins. New York: Farrar, Straus & Giroux, 1971.

Perry, Steve. Push Has Come to Shove: Getting Our Kids the Education They Deserve—Even If It Means Picking a Fight. New York: Crown/Random House, 2011.

Peters, Eugene H. [epilogue by Charles Hartshorne]. The Creative Advance: An Introduction to Process Philosophy as a Context for Christian Faith. St. Louis: Bethany Press, 1966.

Phelps, Janet. "Girl Lobbying for Funding to Fight Cancer." Bryan-College Station Eagle, June 25, 2007. http://archive.theeagle.com/stories/062507/local_20070625024.php.

Polter, Julie. "Education and the Wealth Gap." Sojourners (September–October 2012) 16–19.

Pope, Alexander. An Essay on Criticism, Part III, [1709]. http://www.poetryfoundation.org/resources/learning/essays/detail/69379.

Postman, Neil. The End of Education: Redefining the Value of School. New York: Vintage/Random House, 1995.

Putnam, Robert D. Bowling Alone: The Collapse and Revival of American Community New York: Simon and Schuster, 2000.

Putnam, Robert D., and Lewis M. Feldstein. Better Together: Restoring the American Community. New York: Simon and Schuster, 2003.

Ramsey, Ross. "Analysis: Schools Changing, and Not How You Might Think." Texas Tribune, July 15, 2015. http://www.texastribune.org/2015/07/15/analysis-schools-changing-and-not-how-you-might-th/.

Ravitch, Diane. The Death and Life of The Great American School System: How Testing and Choice Are Undermining Education. New York: Basic Books/Perseus, 2010.

———. "Do Our Public Schools Threaten National Security?" The New York Review of Books June 7, 2012. http://www.nybooks.com/articles/archives/2012/jun/07/do-our-public-schools-threaten-national-security/?pagination=false.

———. The Language Police: How Pressure Groups Restrict What Students Learn. New York: Vintage/Random House, 2003.

———. "The New York Times Hearts Common Core: Susan Ohanian Calls Foul." August 19, 2013. http://dianeravitch.net/2013/08/19/the-new-york-times-hearts-common-core-susan-ohanian-calls-foul/.

———. "Why I Changed My Mind About School Reform." Wall Street Journal, March 9, 2010. http://online.wsj.com/article/SB10001424052748704869304575109443305343962.html.

Rawls, John. Political Liberalism. New York: Columbia University Press, 1993.

Reardon, Sean F. "No Rich Child Left Behind." NYTimes.com, April 29, 2013. http://opinionator.blogs.nytimes.com/2013/04/27/no-rich-child-left-behind/?_r=0.

Rhee, Michelle. Radical: Fighting To Put Students First. New York: Harper Collins, 2013.

Schlechty, Phillip C. Engaging Students: The Next Level of Working on the Work. San Francisco: Jossey-Bass, 2011.

———. Leading for Learning: How to Transform Schools into Learning Organizations. San Francisco: Jossey-Bass, 2009.

Schmolsen, Mike. Focus: Elevating the Essentials to Radically Improve Student Learning. Alexandria, VA: ASCD, 2011.

Schudson, Michael. The Good Citizen: A History of American Civic Life. New York: Free Press, 2011 [reprint].

Self, Nancy. "Total Paradigm Shift Needed to Save K–12 Education in United States." ASCD Express, July 20, 2012. http://www.ascd.org/ascd-express/vol7/720-newvoices.aspx.

Sen, Amartya. "Well Being, Agency, and Freedom: The Dewey Lectures, 1984." Journal of Philosophy 82;4 (April 1985) 169–221. http://www.jstor.org/stable/2026184

Simon, Mark. "High-Stakes Progressive Unionism." In Richard F. Elmore, ed., I Used to Think . . . and Now I Think . . . Twenty Leading Educators Reflect on the Work of School Reform. Cambridge, MA: Harvard Education Press, 2011.

Sizen, Theodore R. Horace's School: Redesigning the American High School. Boston: Houghton Mifflin, 1992.

Skocpol, Theda. Diminished Democracy: From Membership to Management in American Civic Life. Norman: University of Oklahoma Press, 2003.

Slade, Bernard. Tribute. New York: Samuel French, 1978.

Smith, Morgan. "Texas to Apply for No Child Left Behind Waiver." The Texas Tribune, September 6, 2012. http://www.texastribune.org/texas-education/public-education/texas-apply-no-child-left-behind-waiver/.

Texas Association of School Administrators. "Creating a New Vision for Public Education in Texas." Texas Leadership Center. http://www.tasanet.org/cms/lib07/TX01923126/Centricity/Domain/111/workinprogress.pdf.

Texas Classroom Teachers Association. "Resources ≠ Expectations." The Classroom Teacher 32:2 (Summer 2012) 4–8. https://tcta.org/sites/tcta.org/files/publications/SummerMag.pdf.

Thomas-El, Salome, with Cecil Murphy. The Immortality of Influence: We Can Build the Best Minds of the Next Generation. New York: Kensington Pub. Corp., 2006.

Toulouse, Mark G. God in Public: Four Ways American Christianity and Public Life Relate. Louisville, KY: Westminster/JohnKnox, 2006.

Tune, Romal J. "What Can Churches Do? Faith for Change Seeks to Support Public Education—Without Crossing the Church-State Divide." Sojourners (September–October 2012) 24–26.

Webb, Walter Prescott. The Great Frontier. Boston: Houghton-Mifflin, 1952; Austin: University of Texas Press, 1964/1969 [reissue].

Weber, Eric Thomas. "Dewey and Rawls on Education." In Springer Science and Business Media BV 31 (November 25, 2008) 361–82. http://www.jstor.org/stable/40270669.

Weingarten, Randi. "Five Foundations for Student Success." In Weber, Karl, ed. Waiting for Superman: How We Can Save America's Failing Public Schools. New York: Public Affairs/Perseus, 2010.

White, Josh. "Intolerance Found at Air Force Academy." Washington Post, June 22, 2005. http://www.washingtonpost.com/wp-dyn/content/article/2005/06/22/AR2005062200598.html.

Whitehead, Alfred North. The Aims of Education and Other Essays. New York: The Face Press/Simon and Schuster, 1929.

Wilson, Edward O. Conscilience: The Unity of Knowledge. New York: Vintage/ Random House, 1999.

Wilson, Lanford. Talley's Folly. New York: Hill and Wang, 1979.

Wire, Sarah D. "Districts Dispute Facts on Funding: Millage Never Equal, Two Say." Arkansas Democrat-Gazette, December 15, 2012, Arkansas Section, 11.

Wolfe, Alan. Moral Freedom: The Search for Virtue in a World of Choice. New York: W.W. Norton, 2001.

Wuthnow, Robert. Loose Connections: Joining Together in America's Fragmented Communities. Cambridge, MA: Harvard University Press, 1998.

Index

Acts passage, civil engagement
    rationale, 108
African American students, 22,
    92–93
Air Force Academy, 15
Alinsky, Saul D., 100
Amos passage, civil engagement
    rationale, 108
Amplify company, 91
Anglo students, statistics, 22
approach-perspectives, challenge
    categories: authoritarianism,
    55–57; benefits of analyzing,
    47–50; citizen formation,
    60–61; community, 53–54;
    context, 50–51; diagram
    of, 114; innovation, 54;
    needs, 53; personnel, 57–60;
    requirements, 52–53; results,
    50; tradition, 54
Archilochus, 32–33
area-specific schools, 39
Arkansas State Supreme Court,
    82–83
Asian students, statistics, 22
As Texas Goes (Collins), 67–68
authoritarianism challenge,
    approach-perspectives, 55–57
Ayers, William, 10–11

Berlin, Isaiah, 32–33
Berry, Susan, 91
Better Together (Putnam and
    Feldstein), 23–24
biblical interpretations method,
    105–109
Bill and Melinda Gates Foundation,
    71
Blow, Charles, 91–92
Bowling Alone (Putnam), 23, 31
Brimelow, Peter, 68
"broken" quote, 99
Buenger, Erin Channing, 102–103

calling, defined, 7
Calvin, John, 88
caring aspect, sacred calling, 7
CFR (Council on Foreign Relations),
    76–77
change facilitation goal, 44
charter schools, 31, 39–40, 71, 79
cheating, 37–38
choice, school, 26–27, 31, 54–55,
    78–79
Churchill, Winston, 73–74
citizen formation challenge,
    approach-perspectives, 60–61

citizen stakeholders: engagement responsibility, 2, 5–6, 13–14, 16–17, 103; and individualism arguments, 27–30; in meaningful life quest, 9–11; as partnership, 12–13; as positive element of past, 21–23; stewardship aspect, 7–8. *See also* community-building; public, as the main thing

collective associations, 57–58, 68–74. *See also* teachers

Collins, Gail, 67–68

color-changing puzzle comparison, 65

common core curriculum debate, 88–91. *See also* diversity challenges

common good. *See specific topics, e.g.,* democracy; public education, overview

community-building: from Constitution, 25; as positive element of past, 21–23; priority effects, 53–54; purposes, 23–24, 44, 77–78; trade-off aspects, 30–32. *See also* citizen stakeholders; public, as the main thing

competition analogies, 34–36

Constitution, 25, 106

context challenge, approach-perspectives, 50–51

core curriculum debate, 88–91

cost challenge, approach-perspectives, 51

Council on Foreign Relations (CFR), 76–77

Covey, Stephen, 18

"cracked" quote, 99

craft unionism, 72

Darwin, Charles, 93–94

democracy: Alinsky quote, 100; definitions, 12–13;

deliberation's role, 30; education's functions, 12, 27–28, 32; public's role, 10–11, 12–13, 16–17

desegregation orders, approach-perspectives, 54–55

Deuteronomy passage, civil engagement rationale, 108

Dewey, John, 8, 10, 28

Diminished Democracy (Skocpol), 31–32

diversity challenges, 84–90, 92–93. *See also* common core curriculum debate

"do-overs" aphorism, 18–24

The Dream-Keepers (Ladson-Billings), 92–93

Eggers, Dave, 5

electronic devices, approach-perspectives, 54

Eleven Questions, list of, 115–116

empirical standards category, 42–43

The End of Education (Postman), 89

Engaging Students (Hirsch), 78

equalization disputes, 81–84. *See also* financing/funding

equipping students category, 43–44

ethical values, 14–15, 21–23, 105–109

ethnicity patterns, statistics, 22

Eubanks, Fay Shurtleff, 101

facilitating change goal, 44

faith challenge, approach-perspectives, 51–52

Feldstein, Lewis, 23–24

financing/funding: approach-perspectives, 51, 55; complexity issues, 80–84; school types, 38–39, 40, 41–42; teacher effectiveness argument, 5; undermining potential, 79

Index

Fountain Lake School District v. Arkansas Department of Education, 82–83
fox, in hedgehog story, 32–33
Franklin, Benjamin, 25
freedom arguments, 27, 28–30, 31, 87–88
Freedom (Patterson), 28
free market ideology, 41, 66–67, 76–77
Friedman, Matt, 99
Friedman, Milton, 79

Gates Foundation, 71
Gatto, John Taylor, 27, 83, 86–88, 95–96
Goldstein, Dana, 3, 8–9
The Great Frontier (Webb), 32
Green, Charles Leslie, Jr., 26–27

Hartshorne, Charles, 17
"The Hedgehog and the Fox" (Berlin), 32–33
Hegel, Friedrich, 95–96
"hero" quote, 100–101
"High-Stakes Progressive Teacher Unionism" (Simon), 70, 71
Hirsch, E. D., 67, 77, 88–89
Hispanic students, statistics, 22
history, learning from, 18–24
home schooling, 40–41
Houston, Sam, 32
How to Transform Schools into Learning Organizations (Schlechty), 74–75, 77–78
humanistic values, 14–15, 21–23, 105–109

ideology's role, 45, 65–67, 76–77
"if only" statements, 20–21
improvements, possibility factors, 19–20
independent schools, 38–39, 40–41. *See also* choice, school

individualism, 23, 25, 27, 28–31, 86–88
innovation challenge, approach-perspectives, 54
Institutes (Calvin), 88
institution, defined, 12–13
institutional reputation goal, 45
international citizenship, approach-perspectives, 60–61

James passage, civil engagement rationale, 108
Jefferson, Thomas, 32
Jeremiah passage, civil engagement rationale, 108, 109
John passage, civil engagement rationale, 108
1 John passage, civil engagement rationale, 108–109
judicial system, equalization disputes, 81–84
justice, Rawls' arguments, 29–30

Keillor, Garrison, 2–3
Keller, Bill, 90–91
Klein, Joel I., 74, 76–77, 86
Kozol, Jonathan, 81–82

Ladson-Billings, Gloria, 92–93
Lamar, Mirabeau, 32
The Last Dropout (Millican), 6
Leading for Learning (Schlechty), 74–75
legislature, women's health clinics, 37–38
"Let's do it!" quote, 102–103
Leviticus passage, civil engagement rationale, 108
liberal, defined, 13
Lincoln, Abraham, 86–87
low-income households, statistics, 22
Luke passage, civil engagement rationale, 108
Lynn, Ralph, 100

magnet schools, 39
"main thing" aphorism, 18, 27–28, 29–30
Mann, Horace, 27
Mark passage, civil engagement rationale, 108
Marshall, Thurgood, 81–82
Mathews, David, 44, 45
Matthew passage, civil engagement rationale, 108
means-to-end methods, as evaluation strategy, 35–38
means-to-end methods, trajectory effects: diagram of, 113; goals and priorities, 42–46; school types, 38–42. *See also* approach-perspectives
meeting empirical standards goal, 42–43
methodology, author's, 110–112
Micah passage, civil engagement rationale, 108
Millican, Bill, 6
Mitchell, Lloyd, 100–101
Moral Freedom (Wolfe), 31
Moulthrop, Daniel, 5
mudsill theory, 86–87
The Myth of the Common School (Green), 26–27

needs challenge, approach-perspectives, 53
No Child Left Behind program, 42–43, 76
"no do-overs" aphorism, 18–24

occupation *vs.* vocation, 7
Ohanian, Susan, 91
orchestra analogies, 35–36, 48, 49, 65
outsider status, significance, 1–2, 4–5, 13–14, 17, 103. *See also* citizen stakeholders

Palmer, Parker, 9–10
"passion" quote, 101–102
past elements, positive education experiences, 21–23
Patterson, Orlando, 28
Perry, Steve, 68, 74
personal caring aspect, sacred calling, 7
personnel challenge, approach-perspectives, 57–60
picture puzzle comparison, 65
political leverage goal, 45
Political Liberalism (Rawls), 29–30
Pope, Alexander, 103
population statistics, students, 22
Postman, Neil, 68, 89–90
Powell, Lewis, 81–82, 83–84
primers, functions of, 16
private schools, 38–39, 40–41. *See also* choice, school
public, as the main thing, 18, 27–28, 29–32
public education, overview: complexity of goal, 64–65, 97–98; decentralization characteristic, 8–9; as democratic responsibility, 12–13, 16–17, 28, 37; opposition arguments, 26–27; role of people investments, 2–3, 5–6. *See also specific topics, e.g.,* approach perspectives; citizen stakeholders; teachers
public schools, private schools distinction, 38–39
Push Has Come to Shove (Perry), 74
Putnam, Robert, 23–24, 30–31
puzzle comparison, 65

INDEX

"Race to the Top" program, 42, 76
Ravitch, Diane (writing on):
    accountability goal,
    75; charter schools, 71,
    79; citizen literacy, 27;
    distractions, 64–65; historical
    representations, 21, 23;
    ideologies, 66–67, 76–77;
    respect needs, 70
Rawls, John, 28, 29–30
Reclaiming Public Education . . .
    (Mathews), 44
"red-letter-grade day" quote, 101
religious communities and values,
    14–17, 51–52, 88, 94,
    105–109
republic, defined, 13
requirements challenge, approach-
    perspectives, 52–53
research methodology, author's, 2,
    4–5, 110–112
respect, 11, 21–23, 68, 70
results challenge, approach-
    perspectives, 50
results-driven philosophies, 74–78
Rhee, Michelle, 70–71, 74, 85–86
Rice, Condoleezza, 76–77
Rodriguez case, court rulings, 81–82
"The Role of Government in
    Education" (Friedman), 79
Rules for Radicals (Alinsky), 100

sacred calling, overview, 7–8, 14–15.
    See also specific topics, e.g.,
    community-building;
    financing/funding; teachers
Savage Inequalities (Kozol), 81
Schlechty, Phillip, 74–75, 77–78
school choice, 26–27, 31, 54–55, 78–
    79. *See also* charter schools
The Schools We Need (Hirsch), 89
school types, overview, 38–41
Schudson, Michael, 30–31

sectarianism, liabilities summarized,
    14–15
secular values and religious values,
    105–109
select schools, 40, 78–79
Simon, Mark, 70, 72
Skocpol, Theda, 31–32
Slade, Bernard, 101–102
social capital, 21–24
social Darwinism arguments, 93–97
socio-economic statistics, 22
specialty schools, 40
STEM schools, approach-
    perspectives, 60–61
stewardship aspect, sacred calling,
    7–8
Supreme Court ruling, funding
    policy, 81–82

Talley's Folly (Wilson), 99
taxes. *See* financing/funding
teachers: evaluation debates,
    42–43, 57–60, 74–78; as
    intelligent actors, 3–4, 8–9; in
    meaningful life quest, 9–11;
    partnership role, 68–74;
    power of effectiveness, 5
The Teacher Wars (Goldstein), 3, 8–9
Teach for America (TFA), 51, 59
Templeton, Scottie, 101–102
tenure, teacher, 3, 58, 70–71
test-based accountability, 42–43,
    66–67, 74–78
Texas schools, statistics, 21–22
TFA (Teach for America), 51, 59
time, momentum's implications,
    18–21
Tolstoy, Leo, 32–33
tradition challenge, approach-
    perspectives, 54
Tribute (Slade), 101–102
Twenty Questions game, 63–64

undivided life, Palmer's
encouragement, 9–10
unions, 57–58, 68–74. *See also*
teachers
"US Education Reform and National
Security" (Klein, et al.),
76–77

values arguments, 14–15, 26–27,
105–109
virus answer, ideology question,
67–68
vitamin ideology, 67–68
vocation *vs.* occupation, 7

vouchers, 41–42, 79. *See also* charter
schools

Waiting for Superman, 73
"War on the Core" (Keller), 90–91
wasting time, impact, 20–21
Webb, Walter Prescott, 32
Weingarten, Randi, 70, 73
West, Cornel, 89–90
Whitehead, Alfred North, 19, 43–44
Wilson, Lanford, 99
Wolfe, Alan, 31, 41
women's health clinics, 37–38

www.ingramcontent.com/pod-product-compliance
Lightning Source LLC
Chambersburg PA
CBHW072156270326
41930CB00011B/2445